Cambrai 1917

The birth of armoured warfare

Campaign • 187

Cambrai 1917

The birth of armoured warfare

Alexander Turner • Illustrated by Peter Dennis

First published in Great Britain in 2007 by Osprey Publishing,
Midland House, West Way, Botley, Oxford OX2 0PH, UK
443 Park Avenue South, New York, NY 10016, USA
E-mail: info@ospreypublishing.com

A CIP catalogue record for this book is available from the British Library.

ISBN 978 1 84603 147 2

Editorial by Ilios Publishing Ltd, Oxford, UK (www.iliospublishing.com)
Page layout by The Black Spot
Index by Alan Thatcher
Typeset in Helvetica Neue and ITC New Baskerville
Maps by the Map Studio Ltd
3D bird's-eye views by The Black Spot
Battlescene illustrations by Peter Dennis
Originated by United Graphics Pte Ltd, Singapore
Printed in China through World Print Ltd

08 09 10 11 12   11 10 9 8 7 6 5 4 3 2

FOR A CATALOGUE OF ALL BOOKS PUBLISHED BY OSPREY MILITARY AND
AVIATION PLEASE CONTACT:
NORTH AMERICA
Osprey Direct, c/o Random House Distribution Center, 400 Hahn Road,
Westminster, MD 21157
E-mail: info@ospreydirect.com
ALL OTHER REGIONS
Osprey Direct UK, P.O. Box 140 Wellingborough, Northants, NN8 2FA, UK
E-mail: info@ospreydirect.co.uk

www.ospreypublishing.com

FRONT COVER 'Hyacinth' (Male H45 commanded by 2nd Lieutenant
F. H. Jackson) stuck on Hindenburg Support Line west of Ribecourt
on 20 November 1917. Attendant infantry are from the 71st Brigade
of 6th Division. (IWM Q 6432)
TITLE PAGE **A Female Mark IV from the perspective of a defending**
German trench occupant: inhuman and invulnerable. The reality was
very different. (IWM Q 6284)

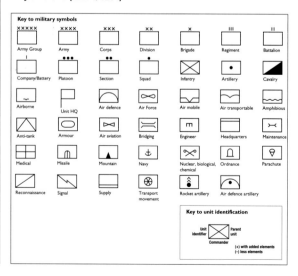

Dedication

Dedicated to the memory of Lance-Corporal Ian Malone and
Piper Christopher Muzvuru, Irish Guards; killed in action in Basra
on Sunday 6 April 2003. *Quis Separabit.*

Acknowledgements

As the aphorism goes, 'history is merely the rearrangement of other
people's words' so I am grateful for all the scholarship, military
report writing and journal keeping that made this exercise possible.
David Fletcher and Janice Tait at the Bovington Tank Museum
Library were especially helpful in navigating me around that
first-class resource. As always, the staff at the Imperial War
Museum and National Archives were exemplary. Thanks also to:
Vince McEllin and Don Kearney at Regimental Headquarters Irish
Guards, Crispin Daly for wading through the German official history
and its indecipherable Gothic script, Peter Dennis for his infectious
enthusiasm and the editor Marcus Cowper for putting up with my
opinions well into the early hours.

Author's note

In describing military formations the text of this narrative conforms
to the convention of only using capital letters in the formal titles
of units. Generic references to corps, divisions, brigades and
regiments etc. remain in the lower case as demonstrated here.
Where denoting a numbered battalion within a regiment, it will
read (for example) 7th/Black Watch. Regional affiliations with
British divisions will only be specified the first time that formation
is mentioned. German words are expressed in italics. Unless part
of the author's collection, all photographs are reproduced with
the kind permission of the Imperial War Museum, Tank Museum
Bovington or Regimental Headquarters Irish Guards.

Imperial War Museum Collections

Many of the photos in this book come from the Imperial War
Museum's huge collections which cover all aspects of conflict
involving Britain and the Commonwealth since the start of the
twentieth century. These rich resources are available online to
search, browse and buy at www.iwmcollections.org.uk. In addition
to Collections Online, you can visit the Visitor Rooms where you
can explore over 8 million photographs, thousands of hours of
moving images, the largest sound archive of its kind in the world,
thousands of diaries and letters written by people in wartime,
and a huge reference library. To make an appointment, call
(020) 7416 5320, or e-mail mail@iwm.org.uk. Imperial War Museum
www.iwm.org.uk

Artist's note

Readers may care to note that the original paintings from which the
colour plates in this book were prepared are available for private
sale. The Publishers retain all reproduction copyright whatsoever.
All enquiries should be addressed to:

Peter Dennis, The Park, Mansfield, Notts, NG18 2AT

The Publishers regret that they can enter into no correspondence
upon this matter.

CONTENTS

THIRD ARMY OBJECTIVES FOR THE CAMBRAI OPERATION

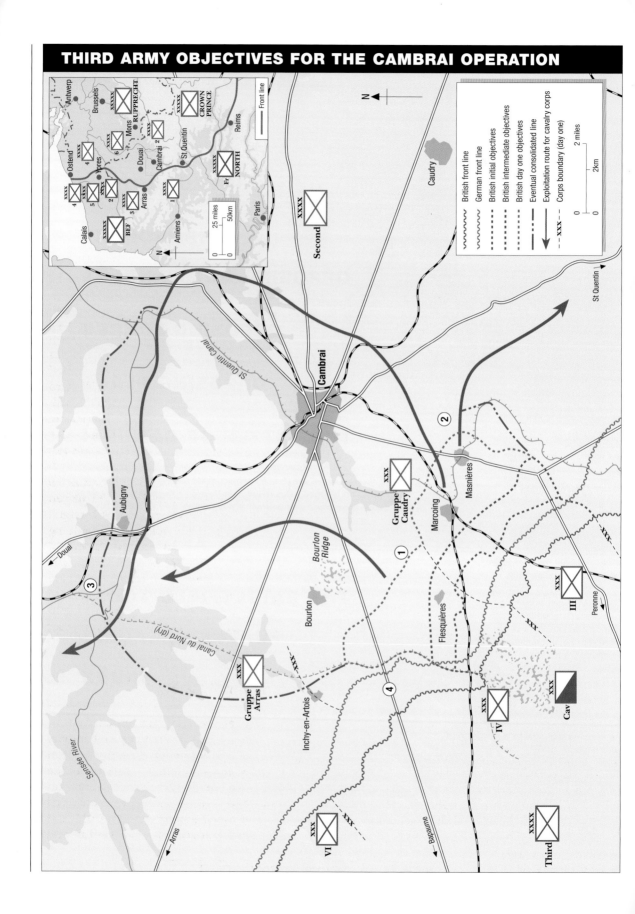

Map legend:
- British front line
- German front line
- British initial objectives
- British intermediate objectives
- British day one objectives
- Eventual consolidated line
- Exploitation route for cavalry corps
- XXX — Corps boundary (day one)

N

0 — 2 miles
0 — 2km

Inset map (BEF sectors):
Antwerp, Brussels, RUPPRECHT, CROWN PRINCE, Ostend, Mons, Reims, Ypres, Douai, Cambrai, St Quentin, Fr NORTH, Calais, Arras, Amiens, Paris, BEF

— Front line

N
0 — 25 miles
0 — 50km

Main map labels:
Second, Caudry, St Quentin, Cambrai, St Quentin Canal, Aubigny, Douai, Gruppe Caudry, Masnières, Marcoing, Bourlon Ridge, Bourlon, Flesquières, Peronne, Gruppe Arras, Inchy-en-Artois, Canal du Nord (dry), Sensée River, III, IV, Cav, VI, Third, Arras, Bapaume

INTRODUCTION

In the front … tanks, manoeuvring back and forth! We pull the ammunition belts from the boxes – our machine gun works itself into a glow and the cooling water hisses. Now a heavy tank has reached the line. It rolls over and away. Some men try to escape. The tank gun stretches them down. One of these wide, dangerous shod wheels drives over the lying wounded Liesenfield, pounding him; pounding his body into the soft ground.[1]

This perception of the tank's emergence onto the battlefields of World War I has, to a large extent, substituted myth for reality. Initially, the metal beasts crawling inexorably across no man's land were a terrible and effective shock to German defenders. Yet events were quick to show that the tank was not destined to be a 'silver bullet' that would break trench deadlock and open up the war on the Western Front. Far from enjoying the invincibility popularly associated with them, early tanks were still defined by their limitations; ponderous, unreliable and surprisingly vulnerable to all forms of enemy fire. Only hindsight confers laurels on a weapon system whose relevance was less than certain at conception.

Nevertheless, whilst the tank's hulking anonymity appears so incompatible with human endeavour, the men inside displayed astonishing fortitude in pursuit of that ever-elusive 'breakthrough'. After early disappointments, they maximized the utility of this budding innovation by harnessing it to the traditional military tenets of coordination, cooperation and training; demonstrating the tank's true promise through kinship with parallel advances in combat aviation and artillery. Rather than complementing existing plans, they sought to employ tanks in an operation that was conceived with these strengths in mind – surprise and concentration of force. At Cambrai in November 1917 the fledgling Tank Corps found their first opportunity.

ORIGINS OF THE CAMPAIGN

The opportunity for an offensive at Cambrai was established by Germany's retirement to the mighty Siegfried Stellung in February 1917. Since the failure of the August 1914 Schlieffen Plan, the German High Command (OHL) had opted for a defensive posture on the Western Front, concentrating instead on defeat of the Russians in the east. Nonetheless, an absolute refusal to accept any territorial withdrawal in the face of sustained Allied attacks through 1915 and 1916 had come at a high price. These extravagances on Verdun and

OPPOSITE **Cambrai's significance as a transport hub is self-evident from this map. Its capture would cause chaos for the German army's logistic effort. The Cambrai battlefield is bounded by the St Quentin Canal to the east and Bourlon Ridge and Sensée River to the north. As the operation was conceived originally as a raid, these limitations on manoeuvre were intended to disrupt German counterattacks. Once Byng and Haig's ambitions for breakthrough entered the equation, they became a liability. Specific objectives (Blue, Brown and Red Lines) were only set for day one (1). Thereafter the planners envisaged a fluid battle of exploitation, with the Cavalry Corps sweeping through a narrow gap to wreak havoc beyond Cambrai (2) and infantry pressing onto Bourlon Ridge. The eventual aim was to consolidate on the Sensée River in order to threaten the entire Hindenburg system north of Cambrai (3). Subsidiary attacks west of the Canal du Nord would protect the flanks of the breach (4).**

1 P. Ettighoffer, *Gespenter am Toten Mann* Bertelsmann: Gütersloh, 1937.

the Somme cost them nearly 750,000 men. Infantry divisions were halved in size to disguise the damage but Germany could not match the Allies' stocks of manpower. The retirement they had resisted for so long became inevitable.

Originally conceived as an insurance policy, the Siegfried Stellung defensive system ran between Arras on the river Scarpe and the Chemin des Dames ridge above the river Aisne, saving 25 miles of front. In manning terms this equated to 13 divisions, precisely the number the Germans needed to create a viable theatre reserve. In the Cambrai area, these defences ran between the prominent obstacles of the St Quentin canal and uncompleted Canal du Nord, which was effectively a deep, dry ditch. Moving north, the line then cut abruptly north-west, across the Canal du Nord, in order to protect the vital rail hub at Cambrai and logistic conduit of the Sensée River. This created a bulge shaped like a nose, with the commanding Bourlon Ridge at its base. Salients always make tempting points to attack because they offer the opportunity to cut off enemy forces with only a modest penetration of their defences. The Cambrai area had added potential because it had not been fought over yet. Its gentle, chalk farmland was firm going and unscarred by shellfire.

This first attracted attention during the Allied spring offensives of April 1917 when the Commander-in-Chief of the British Expeditionary Force (BEF), Field Marshal Sir Douglas Haig, suggested a combined Anglo-French attack on the tempting Cambrai sector. Lieutenant-General Sir William Pulteney's IV Corps was instructed to submit a scheme but, by its completion, preparations for the summer Flanders offensive were well under way. Haig was still enthused by his Cambrai project but Flanders took precedence and General Headquarters (GHQ) shelved Pulteney's work.

Meanwhile, exponents of the tank were busy hatching schemes of their own. The tank's debut at Flers-Courcelette on the Somme in September 1916 had been premature. Though technologically cutting edge, the failing lay in application. In its conception, the tank was a means of protecting infantry and thus it was employed, spread thin as

'an adjunct to infantry attack'. Unfortunately for its advocates, this emphasized the tank's shortcomings. In penny packets, mechanical unreliability had more impact. The tanks bogged down in the quagmire of old battlefields. Without doctrine and training, they failed to integrate with the infantry they were supporting. Despite evident potential, it was an inauspicious beginning.

The first step in rectifying this impasse was the creation of the Tank Corps on 27 July 1917. Hitherto, it had been part of the Machine Gun Corps as its 'Heavy Branch'. Now free to pursue their own doctrine, they were desperate to organize a bespoke operation. They knew that Flanders was the worst possible environment and would only exacerbate the scepticism of senior commanders and fighting infantrymen alike.

Colonel John Fuller (always known by his initials 'J. F. C.'), the now-famous interwar military thinker, was then Chief of Staff to Brigadier-General Hugh Elles, commander of the Tank Corps. He recommended a large-scale raid as the best showcase for their tanks. GHQ turned down an initial suggestion of Neuve Chapelle because of a lack of infantry to support it. Undeterred, Fuller settled on Cambrai as it carried the potential for French involvement, thus addressing the misgiving over lack of infantry. He too saw its favourable setting – perfect for a raid. Bounded by the St Quentin Canal, his proposed force of infantry, tanks, cavalry and aircraft could wreak havoc behind the German front line, whilst protected from counterattack by the canal obstacle.

Their plan secured the interest of Haig and his operations staff but was vetoed by the ever-practical Lieutenant-General Sir Lancelot Kiggell, the Chief of General Staff BEF, on the grounds that it would detract from the ongoing Flanders offensive. However, it also came to the attention of General Sir Julian Byng, recently promoted to command of Third Army off the back of a prodigious spell leading the Canadian Corps in First Army. Third Army had assumed responsibility for the Cambrai sector during June in order to free up forces for Flanders. An imaginative officer, Byng latched onto Fuller's ideas and directed his staff to start incorporating the legacy arrangements inherited from Pulteney.

Bourlon Village viewed from the ridge above. The Sensée River valley can be seen in the distance, proving the significance of Bourlon to British plans for exploitation on a northern axis. (Author's collection)

Coincidentally, the lobbying effort was assisted by yet another proposal for a Cambrai raid, this time from the fertile imagination of Brigadier-General H. H. Tudor, Commander Royal Artillery in 9th Division (part of IV Corps in Byng's Third Army on the Cambrai front). He wanted to test his theories on 'silent registration' of artillery fire by conducting a lightning raid against the Siegfried Stellung in the Flesquières sector.

There was now considerable interest in a Cambrai offensive and Byng took the lead in coordinating the disparate strands into one coherent plan. It was during this process that the parameters of the raid stretched to incorporate contingencies for exploitation. Reacting to intelligence reports that there were, in effect, only two German infantry divisions holding the front at Cambrai, Byng and Elles entertained the possibility of using cavalry to break out before German reserves could be brought in to mount counterattacks. Haig approved of this ambition but, as Byng continued pressing GHQ through September, he was always given the same answer: complete as much preparation as possible without endangering operational security. With the Flanders offensive being renewed, infantry availability remained the principal constraint.

By October, it had become abundantly clear that the limited gains made in Flanders were Pyrrhic at best. Subsidiary attack was the only means of maintaining pressure on the Germans while the French Army rebuilt itself. Furthermore, if Haig did not give Byng the go-ahead imminently, an offensive would not be possible until the New Year. The shortage of infantry could be mitigated by the concentration of an ad hoc theatre reserve under Lieutenant-General Lord Cavan's XIV Corps HQ. Byng would also be given Lieutenant-General Sir Charles Kavanagh's Cavalry Corps and all three brigades of the Tank Corps. On 13 October, Operation *GY* was sanctioned.

The stated aim was 'to break the enemy's defensive system by a *coup de main* … to seize Cambrai, Bourlon Wood, and the passages over the Sensée River and to cut off the troops holding the German front line.'[2]

2 The Third Army Plan for Operation *GY*, issued 13 November 1917.

CHRONOLOGY

1914

3 August – German cavalry patrols enter Belgium at the spearhead of an invading army
August – Battles of Mons, Ardennes and Le Cateau as the BEF and French try to stem the German advance into Belgium and France
September – Allied counterattacks on the Marne, Artois and Aisne drive the Germans back
October – The struggle for manoeuvre culminates in the battle for the Flemish town of Ypres. The hasty defences from Switzerland to the Channel ports solidify through the winter

1915

March – British offensive at Neuve Chapelle. Failure attributed to 'poor communication'
April – Germans initiate second battle of Ypres. Poisonous gas used for the first time
May – British attack at Aubers Ridge and Festubert to no avail while French launch the costly second battle of Artois north of Arras
September–October – British offensive at Loos. First use of the 'creeping barrage'. Battle of Artois continues with a subsidiary French effort east of Reims. Initial success soon gives way to impasse
December – Haig replaces Field Marshal French in command of BEF

1916

February – Germans attempt to draw the French into unsustainable attritional battle by attacking at Verdun. It grinds on, bloody and indecisive, through to June
July – In part to relieve pressure on the French, the British launch their offensive on the Somme. Negligible gains came at horrendous cost but Germany persuaded to suspend Verdun offensive. Falkenhayn replaced in command of German forces by Hindenburg and Ludendorff
July–September – Somme offensive continues with attacks at Delville Wood, Pozières and Thiepval. Tanks used for the first time at Flers-Courcelette on 15 September
October – French counterattack at Verdun
November – Battle of Somme concluded after battle of Ancre. Gains of just seven miles no consolation for 500,000 casualties. Germans lose 420,000
December – At Verdun, the French finally drive the Germans back to where they started. Marshal Joffre replaced at head of French Army by General Nivelle

1917

February – Gross manning pressures compel German withdrawal to Siegfried Stellung (Hindenburg Line). Calais Agreement between Haig and Nivelle on shape of the year's offensive operations
April – America enters the war. Allied joint spring offensive. British attack astride the river Scarpe at Arras. Some spectacular gains, including Vimy Ridge, but pause called after a week. The French effort at the Chemin des Dames makes encouraging early progress but falters after heavy losses. Idea to strike at Cambrai first mooted
May – Both Arras and the Chemin des Dames offensives are concluded. French suffer acts of 'mutiny' and Pétain replaces Nivelle

June – Haig prepares for Flanders offensive by taking Messines Ridge with the detonation of 19 vast mines

July – Third battle of Ypres (Passchendaele) is launched. Early August failures at Gheluvelt Plateau, Langemarck and St Julien are improved by judicious limited operations like Polygon Wood in September. However, having bogged in a rainy quagmire, both Britain and Germany suffer terrible casualties – 400,000 versus 348,000. The offensive is brought to a close in November. Nowhere is the stubborn folly of trench warfare more pronounced

13 October – Third Army Operation *GY* approved by Haig

20 November – Attack commences at Cambrai with stunning initial successes

21 November – Offensive operations resume towards Bourlon, Fontaine, Cantaing and canal crossings at Crèvecoeur

22 November – Germans counterattack Fontaine

23–27 November – Attempts to capture Bourlon Ridge and Fontaine

30 November – German Second Army launches its counterattack across the Cambrai front

1 December – British commence withdrawals. Completed by 7 December

2 December – In the wake of revolution, Russia withdraws from the war under the Treaty of Brest-Litovsk

1918

March – Germans open the *Kaiserschlacht* offensive on the Somme, making huge gains but exhausting their logistic capabilities

April – German subsidiary offensive in Flanders fails as the buttress of Ypres holds firm

May – After a diversionary attack west of the Chemin des Dames, Germany throws itself once more at the French. The biggest advances since 1914 see the Germans pressing against the river Marne once more but overextended forces are checked with the assistance of fresh US divisions

June–July – Further German offensives lack the impetus of early efforts and result in withdrawals

August – Allied counterattacks commence across the entire front. Spent German forces are soon in full retreat. Ludendorff dubs 8 August – the battle of Amiens – his 'black day'

September – Germans have been driven back to their start point on the Siegfried Stellung by the end of the month. US forces make significant gains south-east of Verdun.

October – BEF, French and US armies press home concerted, coordinated offensives across the entire Western Front, breaching German defensive lines routinely. British First Army reaches Mons

11 November – Armistice is signed and the Germans agree to pull back east of the Rhine within 14 days

OPPOSING COMMANDERS

THE BRITISH

Despite its convoluted conception, Byng and Elles were the chief architects of Operation *GY*. Even so, Haig was always in the background. Though he tried to keep a respectful distance from detailed planning, in practice his influence was significant. He controlled the tap on reserves and gave Byng just 48 hours to demonstrate that *GY* was going to achieve its objectives. After the costly obstinacy of Flanders, Haig was conscious not to push his infantry too far. Cambrai represented an opportunity; desirable but not essential to the effort on the Western Front.

In terms of both planning and execution, Cambrai reflects some of the enduring challenges of command in World War I. Of particular pertinence was the integration of emerging technology. It is a common temptation to criticize senior commanders of the period for failing to exploit technologies we now know to be pivotal. Tanks are an excellent example. Their dominance in modern warfare does not necessarily secure their relevance to the conduct of operations in 1917. Myopic as they often appear, commanders were under pressure to win a war. Inevitably, this involved the painful task of prioritizing industrial and military resources. As Paddy Griffith puts it in his study of battle tactics on the Western Front, it was always deemed preferable 'to take a longer but more certain path to victory … than opt for some "death or glory" adventure which ran every chance of failure.'[3] The fluidity of battle imbues all soldiers with a highly developed sense of practicality, placing stock in simplicity of plans, reliability of equipment and sustainability of effort.

Nevertheless, the primary constraint on exploitation of technology was not conceptual. It was the abject inability of commanders to influence events once operations were in progress. Telegraph, field telephones and motorized dispatch aided administration and formulation of planning but were redundant once troops crossed the start line. Thereafter, battlefield communications were little more advanced than in Napoleonic times: runner, bugle, flag, etc. At least the Napoleonic commander was able to survey his battlefield. Trench warfare was a nightmare – diffuse and yet slaved to interdependence with flanking units. By late 1917, the situation had been mitigated by novel solutions like the use of ground marker panels to signal passing aircraft. But these stopgap measures were not extensive enough to alleviate the imperative for prescriptive planning. Only by timetabling events and imposing pauses were commanders able to maintain a semblance of control. The consequence was a catalogue of exasperating lost opportunities.

3 *Battle Tactics of the Western Front*, Paddy Griffith, p. 169.

General Sir Julian Byng. He was a popular and respected figure. D'Oyly Snow, General Officer Commanding VII Corps, recorded Byng's appointment to command of Third Army in his diary: 'I was very glad to hear that they had promoted Bungo. It is very much his show.' (IWM CO 1369)

The innovative Hugh Elles photographed demonstrating his Tank Corps vehicles to King George V in 1918. By then he was a major-general. Ash sticks are carried by Royal Tank Regiment Officers to this day. (Tank Museum 5412/E4)

General the Honourable Sir Julian Byng

It is no coincidence that an operation as seminal as Cambrai had Byng at its head. A commander of noted imagination and thoroughness, he had already masterminded the elite Canadian Corps' efficient capture of Vimy Ridge in April 1917.

Byng was born into the aristocracy, educated at Eton and commissioned into the 10th Hussars. An exemplary record in the colonial campaigns of Sudan and the Second Boer War accelerated his rise through the ranks of Britain's small professional army. In the latter he led an irregular cavalry unit with élan and daring. Deft command of the 3rd Cavalry Division in the dynamic campaigns of summer 1914 earned him promotion and a posting to orchestrate the delicate withdrawal of IX Corps from the Dardanelles in 1915. He was promoted again the following year and assumed command of the Canadian Corps. His evident success in building the reputation of that formation made him a natural choice for command of Third Army when General Allenby left them to command British Forces Egypt in June 1917.

Byng had an affinity with the resourceful Canadians and encouraged many of the enterprising innovations that their officers put to him. Under his aegis, major advances had been made in areas such as the science of artillery counter-battery fire. Therefore when in command of Third Army he was bound to be attracted to the pioneering Elles.

Brigadier-General Hugh Elles

A Royal Engineer by background, Elles was one of many 'Sappers' to be involved in the development of the tank. He was still only a major when posted to the development programme in 1915 but his obvious zeal for this new technology propelled him to the rank of colonel when selected to command of the first tank unit, 'Heavy Branch' Machine Gun Corps in 1916. The formation of the Tank Corps in July 1917 warranted his promotion to brigadier-general at the relatively young age of 37. By attaching himself to such a high-profile procurement project, Elles had risen from obscurity in meteoric fashion – and deservedly so. The BEF is often accused of perpetuating hierarchical strictures but they were no barrier to merit when it mattered.

Mention of Elles would be incomplete without reference to his Chief of Staff, Colonel J. F. C. Fuller. Fuller was an equally passionate devotee of the tank and worked hand-in-hand with Elles to sell its capabilities. He was absolutely fundamental to the creation of written doctrine for use of tanks and, as an infantryman, particularly insistent on a 'combined arms' approach. He went on to be an extremely well-known military thinker whose post-war treatises on armoured warfare heavily influenced the German authors of so-called blitzkrieg doctrine.

THE GERMANS

Though at this stage their contribution to the emergence of armour was negligible, the Germans were adapting well to the new ways of war. Von Moltke's legacy of a highly evolved General Staff to plan, execute and administrate military campaigns was paying dividends in the deliberate logistically demanding environment of trench warfare. They were also extremely flexible.

The *Gruppe* system of creating ad hoc formations from disparate sub-units was genius. It reflected a military culture that, though indisputably rigid in so many ways, always deferred to the person best placed to deliver success on the battlefield. During periods of calm, *Gruppen* built around a corps headquarters were ideally suited to manage the constant state of flux as divisions came in and out of the line. Amidst the chaos of battle, smaller *Gruppen* would form to marshal the remnants of decimated units with lead elements of reinforcing ones. Moreover, when the senior commander of a reinforcing regiment arrived at the front, it was not uncommon for him to subordinate himself to a more junior incumbent with better situational awareness. Cambrai is an exemplar of this command system.

Kronprinz Rupprecht of Bavaria

The western front was split into two by German High Command and Rupprecht was the commander of German Army Group North. Although, as Haig's equivalent, he may seem somewhat remote from events, owing to the importance of reserves to the German conduct of this battle, Rupprecht was instrumental in its outcome. He also planned the counterattacks they went on to launch in response.

Eldest son of Ludwig III, the last King of Bavaria, Rupprecht had a rich pedigree. His full title was 'His Royal Highness Rupprecht Maria Luitpold Ferdinand, Crown Prince of Bavaria, Duke of Bavaria, Franconia and Swabia, Count Palatine of the Rhine'! Initial command of the German Sixth Army in 1914 was a function of his Royal position but a life of study and elevated status had equipped him well for the responsibility. He proved a highly able commander, first checking the August 1914 French counterattack at Lorraine and then managing to mount one of his own. His promotion to command of Army Group North in 1916 was well deserved and he held it until the Armistice in 1919. Having lost his formal powers in the post-war years, he opposed Nazi rule and was forced into exile in 1939.

General von der Marwitz

Byng's counterpart at Cambrai was General Johannes von der Marwitz, commander of the German Second Army. Also a cavalryman, von der Marwitz had a pre-war career split equally between his regiment and the staff. Most of his World War I service was seen on the Eastern Front, where he commanded the XXXVIII Reserve Corps at the winter (second) battle of the Masurian Lakes in Feburary 1915. Decorated *Pour le Mérite* for his service there, he served for a spell in command of VI Corps on the Western Front before returning again to the east in the summer of 1916. Three months as the Kaiser's Adjutant preceded his selection to command Second Army at the end of that year. The fact that von der Marwitz was always being shunted around from one offensive to the next is testament to his standing in the eyes of Germany's High Command.

Kronprinz Rupprecht of Bavaria. His appointment to command of the Germans' northern Army Group on the Western Front owed nothing to nepotism. He was an able commander. (IWM Q 23727)

General von der Marwitz, commander of German Second Army. He was not convinced that the Cambrai sector was at all vulnerable 'because our defensive system is particularly strong'. At the very least, he expected systematic bombardment as warning. (IWM Q 68033)

OPPOSING FORCES

THE GERMANS

Germany's manning respite was short lived. Flanders proved almost as costly for Germany as it was for the BEF – 348,000 casualties versus 397,000 respectively. The divisions saved by the withdrawal to the Siegfried Stellung were largely absorbed by the necessity to raise an army for operations against the Italians in autumn 1917. Success on the Eastern Front was starting to release divisions for the west but in mid-October, these were only just becoming available. The German army was tired and stretched thin. In quiet sectors, units were undermanned and often recuperating from battle. Cambrai was nicknamed the 'Flanders Sanatorium' for its preponderance of combat-weary units.

This parlous state created strategic headaches for Germany, but their fighting men were still a force to be reckoned with. They too had been adapting and innovating. German defensive doctrine was highly developed and wedded to inventions like reinforced concrete. Advances were also being made in the offensive domain with the emergence of *Stosstruppen* – stormtroops.

A great deal of mystique now surrounds these units. In truth, they were simply applying tactical common sense, certainly similar to the infantry doctrine being adopted by the BEF during the same period.

In March 1915, OHL ordered the formation of an experimental unit to test new equipments and tactics. This became the 1st Sturmabteilung Battalion, a training formation. Indeed, all the first *Stosstruppen* units

Stosstruppen training with a flame-thrower. The essence of their tactics was orchestration of manoeuvre and firepower. Man-portable weapons like this one were favoured because they were organic to local commanders and so could be employed exactly when and where needed for best effect. (IWM Q 55426)

were formed to spread best practice. Officers and non-commissioned officers (NCOs) were posted for short periods in order to gain experiences they could pass on to their regiments. But unlike the BEF, which was attempting much the same thing with its centralized battle schools, *Stosstruppen* units were active fighting formations that spearheaded local raids and offensives. Once they had demonstrated their worth, the idea spread. By October 1916, every army commander on the Western Front was ordered to raise a *Sturmbataillon*. As intended, it became a culture that infantrymen aspired to. Recruits had to have an exemplary record, both in terms of discipline and fitness. These procedures are what have spawned the elite reputation of *Sturmbataillone* but even in late 1917 such men were in very short supply. Most German infantry had a rather more mundane existence.

The forces facing Operation *GY* at Cambrai were part of Gruppe Caudry, one of three such formations in von der Marwitz's Second Army (the others being Gruppen Arras and Quentin). Gruppe Caudry was based around XIII Corps headquarters, under the command of General Freiherr von Watter. It contained four infantry divisions: the 20th Landwehr in the north, 54th Infantry and 9th Reserve Infantry in the centre and 183rd Infantry Division in the far south. The 20th Landwehr was relieving the 204th Infantry Division; a process not completed until 12 November.

By this stage, the pre-war categorizations of 'Reserve Infantry' and '*Landwehr*' effectively had lost their meaning; all infantry divisions were manned and equipped on similar lines. They had also shed brigade structures as part of the 1916 manpower reduction. A division now fielded three regiments, which were subdivided into three battalions, each of four companies. The company was the basic manoeuvre element, especially in defence. Established for 264 men, in practice they mustered nearer 150. Casualties and sickness had taken their toll. Regiments also drew on the rifle companies for the creation of unofficial machine-gun detachments and assault units.

In defence, the regiment was given a portion of the division's frontage and manned it in depth by rotating the three battalions through the front-line, support and reserve trench systems. Given that the reserve positions were beyond the range of enemy field artillery, troops generally lived at rest in billets, fulfilling administrative functions like road repair. They were also earmarked for counterattack if forward positions fell to attack.

When occupying fighting positions, routine in the 'Flanders Sanatorium' was not necessarily baneful. The trenches included dugouts deep enough to resist shelling and foul weather. Foul air and vermin infestations were in the bargain but the stolid infantrymen were used to that. Quality of life really depended on the aggressiveness of the British unit opposite – some raided and harassed more than others.

THE BRITISH

Given the modest size of its pre-war nucleus, the 1.5-million-strong BEF of 1917 was a remarkable entity. Expansion occurred in concert with rapid progress across the sphere of military capability from munitions to military medicine. The pace of change during World War I was unprecedented in military history. Generals that had started their military careers using single-shot weapons and infantry squares were now able to call upon the likes of aerial photoreconnaissance, chemical weapons and tanks.

Some of the most astonishing developments are to be found in the realm of airpower and artillery. The Royal Flying Corps deployed to France in August 1914 with 50 light observation aircraft. By November 1917, they were operating a mixed force of 1,000 fighters, bombers, and reconnaissance aircraft. Many of the latter were being used to adjust the fire of long-range artillery; a capability not superseded until the advent of unmanned drones some 80 years later.

By late 1917, British artillery was becoming remarkably sophisticated. 18-pdr field artillery batteries like this one were the workhorses, delivering stunningly precise creeping barrages to protect advancing infantry. Camouflage awnings are in place to defeat balloon observation. (IWM Q 2247)

Indeed, modern artillery owes much to that frenetic period of modernization. Artillerymen started the war in expectation of firing at targets in line of sight but were soon perfecting the science of indirect fire using distant observers, variable charges and complex fuses. Meteorology, metallurgy and trigonometry all became essential disciplines in achieving accuracy over escalating distances. Scientists perfected flash spotting and sound ranging methods for locating enemy gun batteries to within 10m. Infantry were protected in the assault by a 'creeping barrage' of light field gun shells that laid a curtain of fire as little as 75m ahead. Impressive as this was, the dominance of artillery provoked an equal and opposite reaction from the men creating field fortifications. Their efforts required ever-increasing preparatory bombardment; always to the detriment of surprise. Thus forewarned, defenders then had their reserves primed to preclude disaster.

The arrival of the tank was an encouraging development. It could crush barbed wire, which hitherto had proved the most problematic preparatory task. However, all the accompanying missions like counter-battery fire and 'standing' barrage of depth targets still required 'registration' – the process of adjusting rounds onto the target. This is necessary because rounds seldom hit the target first time. Weather conditions, ammunition batches and gun barrel temperatures always differ. Complete surprise could only be achieved if the artillery was able to refine nascent techniques for registering without firing.

Brigadier-General Tudor already harboured ambition for this 'silent registration' and Byng was keen to develop it. Essentially, the process involved firing purely by map. Exceptional cartography and thorough survey of gun positions were the key prerequisites. Data was also compiled for atmospheric effects on artillery rounds, muzzle velocities and barrel wear rates. With all the key variables covered in this way, mathematical prediction of impact was feasible.

The prospect of genuine surprise was tantalizing. It was now down to the tanks to get the infantry through the wire. Protection of infantry in the assault presented the most intractable conundrum of the war. Even a single machine gun had sufficient reach and lethality to hold up a battalion. As previously mentioned, the creeping barrage had proved its worth in shielding advancing infantry but its inflexible timetabling could also be a liability. Troops often either paused needlessly or lagged too far behind. In theory, some kind of off-road armoured vehicle could address most of these issues.

It is beyond the scope of this Campaign title to chart the development of the tank. Any of David Fletcher's works (see Further reading) will inform with abundant detail and anecdotal colour. Suffice it to say, it was an outstanding engineering accomplishment. From the initiation of the 'Landship' Committee in February 1915, it took them just seven months to build a working prototype. Thirty-two tanks went into battle for the first time as C and D Companies of Heavy Branch, Machine Gun Corps at Flers-Courcelette on 15 September 1916. By November 1917 the tank was on its fourth iteration, incorporating many design improvements.

The Mark IV tank came in two mechanically identical forms: Male and Female. Male variants were armed with two Lewis light machine guns and two Hotchkiss naval quick-firing 6-pdr guns in the side sponsons, whereas the Female just mounted four Lewis guns instead.

This fearsome wire entanglement has been contrived to demonstrate the Mark IV's capabilities. F1 is a Female variant with two Lewis guns protruding from each sponson. She is also bearing a supply of 'Spuds' – track attachments that increased the width and therefore, grip. One can be seen fitted on the front right. They proved impractical, picking up wire and dragging it along. (IWM Q 6424)

Originally, this reflected a shortage of 6-pdrs but Females proved their utility because machine guns were able to fire on the move – something impossible for the 6-pdr owing to transmission vibrations disturbing its sights. All variants had one forward-firing and (notionally) one rear-firing Lewis. Target acquisition was limited by narrow vision slits.

With an optimistic top speed of 3.7mph, the Mark IV was never in a hurry. Direction changing was so complicated that it could take up to five minutes to pull a U-turn. Very minor adjustments could be made by the driver applying one of the track brakes but the only totally practical method was for the tank to stop, lock its differential and get the gearsmen in the back to engage (or disengage) secondary gears so that only one track was then under power.

In terms of protection, the armour plate on tanks of this period was nowhere near as advanced as it is today. These early designs did not incorporate the advantages to be gained by sloping armour, nor had they mastered the ability to 'face harden' rolled steel, thus leaving the inside much less brittle. Consequently, early tanks suffered terribly from 'spall' – jagged pieces of steel being knocked off the inside of armour by a bullet strike to the outside. The Mark IV was not proof against armour-piercing rifle ammunition and any hit from a direct-fire artillery round would generally prove catastrophic. Enemy infantry also soon learnt to fire at vision slits. This created an effect that crews called 'splash' – ricochets and fragments of copper bullet jacket whizzing into the tank's interior.

Fire was a terrifyingly realistic prospect. Rear-mounted external petrol tanks were fairly vulnerable but crews also perched astride the engine and transmission. There were no firewalls or baffles to protect them. Airspaces were thick with fuel vapour; worse yet, canvas coveralls were saturated with oil and petrol. The final moments of many a crew were captured by a cluster of immolated remains around inadequate egress hatches.

In fact, life for a tank crew was unpleasant in most respects. Though half the width and weight of a modern four-man Main Battle Tank, the Mark IV squeezed in eight men: commander, driver, two gunners, two loaders and the two gearsmen in the back. Once inside and 'closed down', the Stygian gloom was penetrated only by a few dim lamps and shafts of light from vision slits. The engine was so noisy that

communication was impossible except by hand signal. Lacking any form of suspension, the ride was literally bone jarring. Temperatures soared quickly to 50 degrees Celsius (120 Fahrenheit), irrespective of conditions outside. Fumes from the engine and weapons systems created a noxious cocktail of petrol vapour, carbon monoxide, oil smoke and cordite. It was perfectly normal for crewmen to pass out. Current health and safety legislation would not permit five minutes in these conditions. Tank Corps crews in 1917 regularly tolerated seven to eight hours. Service with the Tank Corps was no easy ride.

Nevertheless, casualty rates were broadly still lower than the infantrymen they were supporting. Then, as now, defences could only be cleared and consolidated by the feral aggression of men with rifles, grenades and bayonets. Akin to the German army, BEF infantry tactics had reached significant maturity.

The cornerstone of this new doctrine was 'fire and movement'. Thirty-six-man infantry platoons were balanced to create an assault element, suppression elements and a reserve. Once presented with a specific objective, the platoon would lay down suppressive fire with its Lewis light machine gun (supported by eight ammunition bearers) and a nine-man section of 'rifle bombers'. The assault section (nine 'bombers' equipped with hand grenades) could then work their way around to an exposed flank and clear the position. A mixed reserve section sat with the command element in preparation to support either function as necessary. This basic procedure has not changed since. Indeed, an infantryman from 1917 would assimilate modern infantry weapons and tactics with ease.

ORDERS OF BATTLE

Note: Vital as they were, space precludes detailing formation support units such as aircraft, artillery, engineers, pioneer, cavalry and logistics. This information is readily available in the National Archives records, Official Histories or by correspondence with the author.

BRITISH

THIRD ARMY – Gen. Hon Sir J. H. G. Byng

III CORPS – Lt. Gen. Sir W. P. Pulteney

6th Division – Maj. Gen. T. O. Marden
16th Infantry Brigade – Brig. Gen. H. A. Walker
8th Battalion Bedfordshire Regiment
2nd Battalion York and Lancaster Regiment
1st Battalion King's Shropshire Light Infantry
1st Battalion East Kent Regiment 'Buffs'
18th Infantry Brigade – Brig. Gen. G. S. G. Craufurd
1st Battalion West Yorkshire Regiment
2nd Battalion Durham Light Infantry
14th Battalion Durham Light Infantry
11th Battalion Essex Regiment (attached to 71st Bde. for GY)
71st Infantry Brigade – Brig. Gen. P. W. Brown
1st Battalion Leicestershire Regiment
9th Battalion Suffolk Regiment
9th Battalion Norfolk Regiment
2nd Battalion Sherwood Foresters

20th (Light) Division – Maj. Gen. W. Douglas Smith
59th Infantry Brigade – Brig. Gen. H. H. G. Hyslop
10th Battalion Rifle Brigade
11th Battalion Rifle Brigade
10th Battalion King's Royal Rifle Corps
11th Battalion King's Royal Rifle Corps
60th Infantry Brigade – Brig. Gen. F. J. Duncan
12th Battalion Rifle Brigade
12th Battalion King's Royal Rifle Corps
6th Battalion Oxfordshire and Buckinghamshire Light Infantry
6th Battalion King's Shropshire Light Infantry
61st Infantry Brigade – Brig. Gen. W. E. Banbury
7th Battalion Duke of Cornwall's Light Infantry
7th Battalion Somerset Light Infantry
7th Battalion King's Own Yorkshire Light Infantry
12th Battalion Liverpool Regiment (King's)

12th (Eastern) Division – Maj. Gen. A. B. Scott
35th Infantry Brigade – Brig. Gen. B. Vincent
9th Battalion Essex Regiment
7th Battalion Suffolk Regiment
5th Battalion Royal Berkshire Regiment
7th Battalion Norfolk Regiment
36th Infantry Brigade – Brig. Gen. C. S. Owen
7th Battalion Sussex Regiment
8th Battalion Royal Fusiliers (City of London)
9th Battalion Royal Fusiliers (City of London)
11th Battalion Middlesex Regiment
37th Infantry Brigade – Brig. Gen. A. B. Incledon-Weber
7th Battalion East Surrey Regiment
6th Battalion East Kent Regiment 'Buffs'
6th Battalion Royal West Kent Regiment (Queen's Own)
6th Battalion Royal West Surrey Regiment (Queen's)

29th Division – Maj. Gen. Sir H. de Beauvoir de Lisle
86th Infantry Brigade – Brig. Gen. G. R. H. Cheape
1st Battalion Royal Guernsey Light Infantry
1st Battalion Lancashire Fusiliers
2nd Battalion Royal Fusiliers (City of London)
16th Battalion Middlesex Regiment

87th Infantry Brigade – Brig. Gen. C. H. T. Lucas
1st Battalion King's Own Borderers
1st Battalion Border Regiment
1st Battalion Lancashire Fusiliers
2nd Battalion South Wales Borderers
88th Infantry Brigade – Brig. Gen. H. Nelson
1st Battalion Essex Regiment
1st Battalion Newfoundland Regiment
2nd Battalion Hampshire Regiment
4th Battalion Worcestershire Regiment

IV CORPS – Lt. Gen. Sir C. L. Woollcombe

36th (Ulster) Division – Maj. Gen. O. S. W. Nugent
107th Infantry Brigade – Brig. Gen. W. N. Withycombe
8th Battalion Royal Irish Rifles
9th Battalion Royal Irish Rifles
10th Battalion Royal Irish Rifles
1st Battalion Royal Irish Fusiliers
108th Infantry Brigade – Brig. Gen. C. R. J. Griffith
11th Battalion Royal Irish Rifles
12th Battalion Royal Irish Rifles
13th Battalion Royal Irish Rifles
9th Battalion Royal Irish Fusiliers
109th Infantry Brigade – Brig. Gen. A. St Q. Ricardo
9th Battalion Royal Inniskilling Fusiliers
10th Battalion Royal Inniskilling Fusiliers
11th Battalion Royal Inniskilling Fusiliers
14th Battalion Royal Irish Rifles

51st (Highland) Division – Maj. Gen. G. M. Harper
152nd Infantry Brigade – Brig. Gen. H. P. Burn
5th Battalion Seaforth Highlanders
6th Battalion Seaforth Highlanders
6th Battalion Gordon Highlanders
8th Battalion Argyll and Sutherland Highlanders
153rd Infantry Brigade – Brig. Gen. A. T. Beckwith
5th Battalion Gordon Highlanders
7th Battalion Gordon Highlanders
6th Battalion Black Watch
7th Battalion Black Watch
154th Infantry Brigade – Brig. Gen. K. G. Buchanan
4th Battalion Gordon Highlanders
4th Battalion Seaforth Highlanders
7th Battalion Argyll and Sutherland Highlanders
9th Battalion Royal Scots

62nd (West Riding) Division – Maj. Gen. Sir W. P. Braithwaite
185th Infantry Brigade – Brig. Gen. Viscount Hampden
5th Battalion West Yorkshire Regiment
6th Battalion West Yorkshire Regiment
7th Battalion West Yorkshire Regiment
8th Battalion West Yorkshire Regiment
186th Infantry Brigade – Brig. Gen. R. B. Bradford VC
4th Battalion Duke of Wellington's Regiment
5th Battalion Duke of Wellington's Regiment
6th Battalion Duke of Wellington's Regiment
7th Battalion Duke of Wellington's Regiment
187th Infantry Brigade – Brig. Gen. R. O'B. Taylor
4th Battalion King's Own Yorkshire Light Infantry
5th Battalion King's Own Yorkshire Light Infantry
4th Battalion York and Lancaster Regiment
5th Battalion York and Lancaster Regiment

CAVALRY CORPS – Lt. Gen. C. T. McM. Kavanagh

1st Cavalry Division – Maj. Gen. R. L. Mullens
1st Cavalry Brigade – Brig. Gen. E. Makins
2nd Dragoon Guards (Queen's Bays)
5th Dragoon Guards (Princess Charlotte of Wales')
11th Hussars (Prince Albert's Own)

2nd Cavalry Brigade – Brig. Gen. D. J. E. Beale-Brown
 4th Dragoon Guards (Royal Irish)
 9th Lancers (Queen's Royal)
 18th Hussars (Queen Mary's Own)
9th Cavalry Brigade – Brig. Gen. D'A. Legard
 1st Bedfordshire Yeomanry
 15th Hussars (The King's)
 19th Hussars (Queen Alexandra's Own Royal)

2nd Cavalry Division – Maj. Gen. W. H. Greenly
3rd Cavalry Brigade – n/k
 4th Hussars (Queen's Own)
 5th Lancers (Royal Irish)
 16th Lancers (The Queen's)
4th Cavalry Brigade – n/k
 6th Dragoon Guards (Carabiniers)
 3rd Hussars (King's Own)
 1st Oxfordshire Yeomanry
5th Cavalry Brigade – Brig. Gen. C. L. K. Campbell
 2nd Dragoons (Royal Scots Greys)
 12th Lancers (Prince of Wales' Own Royal)
 20th Hussars

3rd Cavalry Division – Brig. Gen. A. E. W. Harman
6th Cavalry Brigade – n/k
 3rd Dragoon Guards (Prince of Wales')
 1st Royal Dragoons
 1st North Somerset Yeomanry
7th Cavalry Brigade – n/k
 1st Life Guards
 2nd Life Guards
 Royal Horse Guards
8th Cavalry Brigade – n/k
 10th Hussars (Prince of Wales' Own Royal)
 1st Essex Yeomanry

4th Cavalry Division – Maj. Gen. A. A. Kennedy
Sialkot Cavalry Brigade – n/k
 17th Lancers (Duke of Cambridge's Own)
 6th Cavalry (King Edward's Own)
 19th Lancers (Fane's Horse)
Mhow Cavalry Brigade – Brig. Gen. N. M. Haig
 2nd Lancers (Gardner's Horse)
 38th Central India Horse (King George's Own)
 6th Inniskilling Dragoons
Lucknow Cavalry Brigade – Brig. Gen. M. F. Gage
 36th Jacob's Horse
 Jodhpur Lancers
 29th Lancers (Deccan Horse)

5th Cavalry Division – Maj. Gen. H. J. M. MacAndrew
Ambala Cavalry Brigade – Brig. Gen. C. H. Rankin
 8th Hussars (King's Royal Irish)
 9th Lancers (Hodson's Horse)
 18th Lancers (King George's Own)
Secunderabad Cavalry Brigade – n/k
 7th Dragoon Guards (Princess Royal's)
 34th Poona Horse
 20th Lancers (Deccan Horse)
Canadian Cavalry Brigade – Brig. Gen. J. E. B. Seely
 Lord Strathcona's Horse
 Fort Garry Horse
 Royal Canadian Dragoons

TANK CORPS – Brig. Gen. H. J. Elles
I Tank Brigade – Col. C. D'A. B. S. Baker Carr
 D Battalion Tank Corps
 E Battalion Tank Corps
 G Battalion Tank Corps
II Tank Brigade – Col. A. Courage
 A Battalion Tank Corps
 B Battalion Tank Corps
 H Battalion Tank Corps
III Tank Brigade – Col. J. Hardress-Lloyd
 C Battalion Tank Corps
 F Battalion Tank Corps
 I Battalion Tank Corps

Units in action from 23 November:

Guards Division – Maj. Gen. G. P. T. Feilding
1st Guards Brigade – Brig. Gen. C. R. Champion de Crespigny
 2nd Battalion Grenadier Guards
 2nd Battalion Coldstream Guards
 3rd Battalion Coldstream Guards
 1st Battalion Irish Guards
2nd Guards Brigade – Brig. Gen. B. N. Sergison Brooke
 3rd Battalion Grenadier Guards
 1st Battalion Coldstream Guards
 1st Battalion Scots Guards
 2nd Battalion Irish Guards
3rd Guards Brigade – Brig. Gen. Lord Seymour
 1st Battalion Grenadier Guards
 4th Battalion Grenadier Guards
 2nd Battalion Scots Guards
 1st Battalion Welsh Guards

40th Division – Maj. Gen. J Ponsonby
119th Infantry Brigade – Brig. Gen. F. P. Crozier
 19th Battalion Royal Welch Fusiliers
 12th Battalion South Wales Borderers
 17th Battalion Welsh Regiment
 18th Battalion Welsh Regiment
120th Infantry Brigade – n/k
 13th Battalion East Surrey Regiment
 14th Battalion Highland Light Infantry
 14th Battalion Argyll and Sutherland Highlanders
 11th Battalion Royal Lancaster Regiment (King's Own)
121st Infantry Brigade – Brig. Gen. J. Campbell
 12th Battalion Suffolk Regiment
 13th Battalion Yorkshire Regiment
 20th Battalion Middlesex Regiment
 21st Battalion Middlesex Regiment

56th (1st London) Division – Maj. Gen. F. A. Dudgeon
167th Infantry Brigade – Brig. Gen. G. H. B. Freeth
 1st Battalion Royal Fusiliers (City of London)
 3rd Battalion Royal Fusiliers (City of London)
 7th Battalion Middlesex Regiment
 8th Battalion Middlesex Regiment
168th Infantry Brigade – n/k
 4th Battalion Royal Fusiliers (City of London)
 12th Battalion London Regiment (The Rangers)
 13th Battalion London Regiment (Kensington)
 14th Battalion London Regiment (London Scottish)
169th Infantry Brigade – Brig Gen E. S. D'E. Coke
 2nd Battalion Royal Fusillers (City of London)
 5th Battalion London Regiment (London Rifle Brigade)
 9th Battalion London Regiment (Queen's Victoria Rifles)
 16th Battalion London Regiment (Queen's Westminster Rifles)

2nd Division – Maj. Gen. C. E. Pereira
5th Infantry Brigade – Brig. Gen. W. Bullen Smith
 2nd Battalion Oxfordshire and Buckinghamshire Light Infantry
 2nd Battalion Highland Light Infantry
 17th Battalion Royal Fusiliers (City of London)
 24th Battalion Royal Fusiliers (City of London)
6th Infantry Brigade – Brig. Gen. R. K. Walsh
 1st Battalion King's Regiment (Liverpool)
 2nd Battalion South Staffordshire Regiment
 13th Battalion Essex Regiment
 17th Battalion Middlesex Regiment
99th Infantry Brigade – Brig. Gen. R. O. Kellett
 1st Battalion King's Royal Rifle Corps
 1st Battalion Royal Berkshire Regiment
 22nd Battalion Royal Fusiliers (City of London)
 23rd Battalion Royal Fusiliers (City of London)

47th (2nd London) Division – Maj. Gen. G. F. Gorringe
140th Infantry Brigade – Brig. Gen. H. P. B. L. Kennedy
 6th Battalion London Regiment (City of London Rifles)
 7th Battalion London Regiment (City of London)
 8th Battalion London Regiment (Post Office Rifles)
 15th Battalion London Regiment (Civil Service Rifles)
141st Infantry Brigade – Brig. Gen. J. F. Erskine
 17th Battalion London Regiment (Poplar and Stepney Rifles)

18th Battalion London Regiment (London Irish Rifles)
19th Battalion London Regiment (St Pancras)
20th Battalion London Regiment (Blackheath and Woolwich)
142nd Infantry Brigade – Brig. Gen. V. T. Bailey
21st Battalion London Regiment (1st Surrey Rifles)
22nd Battalion London Regiment (The Queen's)
23rd Battalion London Regiment (County of London)
24th Battalion London Regiment (The Queen's)

55th (West Lancashire) Division – Maj. Gen. H. S. Jeudwine
164th Infantry Brigade – Brig. Gen. C. I. Stockwell
4th Battalion Royal Lancaster Regiment (King's Own)
4th Battalion Royal North Lancaster Regiment
8th Battalion King's Regiment (Liverpool)
5th Battalion Lancashire Fusiliers
165th Infantry Brigade – Brig. Gen. L. B. Boyd Moss
5th Battalion King's Regiment (Liverpool)
6th Battalion King's Regiment (Liverpool)
7th Battalion King's Regiment (Liverpool)
9th Battalion King's Regiment (Liverpool)
166th Infantry Brigade – Brig. Gen. F. G. Lewis
5th Battalion Royal Lancaster Regiment (King's Own)
5th Battalion South Lancashire Regiment
10th Battalion King's Regiment (Liverpool)
5th Battalion Royal North Lancaster Regiment

GERMAN

SECOND ARMY – Gen. von der Marwitz

XIV CORPS – Gruppe Arras – Gen.Lt. von Moser

111th Infantry Division – Gen.Maj. von Busse
73rd Fusilier Regiment
76th Infantry Regiment
164th Infantry Regiment

240th Infantry Division – Gen.Maj. Müller
469th Infantry Regiment
470th Infantry Regiment
471st Infantry Regiment

20th Infantry Division – Gen.Maj. Wellmann
77th Infantry Regiment
79th Infantry Regiment
92nd Infantry Regiment

Added as battle reinforcement or for the 30 November counteroffensive:

3rd Guards Infantry Division – Gen.Maj. von Lindequist
Guard Fusilier Regiment
Lehr Infantry Regiment
9th Grenadier Regiment

21st Reserve Infantry Division – Gen.Maj. Briefe
80th Reserve Infantry Regiment
87th Reserve Infantry Regiment
88th Reserve Infantry Regiment

221st Infantry Division – Gen.Maj. von la Chevallerie
41st Infantry Regiment
60th Reserve Infantry Regiment
1st Ersatz Reserve Infantry Regiment

214th Infantry Division – Gen.Maj. von Brauchitsch
50th Infantry Regiment
358th Infantry Regiment
363rd Infantry Regiment

49th Reserve Infantry Division – Gen.Maj. von Unger
225th Reserve Infantry Regiment
226th Reserve Infantry Regiment
228th Reserve Infantry Regiment

XIII CORPS – Gruppe Caudry – Gen.Lt. von Watter

20th Landwehr Division – Gen.Maj. von Hanstein
384th Landwehr Infantry Regiment
386th Landwehr Infantry Regiment
387th Landwehr Infantry Regiment

54th Infantry Division – Gen.Maj. von Watter
84th Infantry Regiment
27th Reserve Infantry Regiment
90th Reserve Infantry Regiment

9th Reserve Infantry Division – Gen.Maj. von Hildemann
395th Infantry Regiment
6th Reserve Infantry Regiment
19th Reserve Infantry Regiment

183rd Infantry Division – Gen.Maj. von Schüssler
184th Infantry Regiment
418th Infantry Regiment
440th Infantry Regiment

Added as battle reinforcement or for the 30 November counteroffensive:

107th Infantry Division – Gen.Maj. Havenstein
52nd Reserve Infantry Regiment
227th Reserve Infantry Regiment
232nd Reserve Infantry Regiment

119th Infantry Division – Gen.Maj. Berger
46th Infantry Regiment
58th Infantry Regiment
46th Reserve Infantry Regiment

28th Infantry Division – Gen.Maj. Langer
40th Fusilier Regiment
Lieb Grenadier Regiment
110th Grenadier Regiment

30th Infantry Division – Gen.Maj. Freiherr von der Wenge
99th Infantry Regiment
105th Infantry Regiment
143rd Infantry Regiment

220th Infantry Division – Gen.Maj. von Bassewitz
190th Infantry Regiment
55th Reserve Infantry Regiment
99th Reserve Infantry Regiment

Formed for the 30 November counteroffensive:

XXIII CORPS – Gruppe Busigny – Gen.Lt. von Kathen

34th Infantry Division – Gen.Maj. Leezmann
30th Infantry Regiment
67th Infantry Regiment
145th Infantry Regiment

208th Infantry Division – Gen.Maj. von Grodded
25th Infantry Regiment
185th Infantry Regiment
65th Reserve Infantry Regiment

5th Guards Infantry Division – Gen.Maj. von der Often
3rd Guard Regiment
3rd Guard Grenadier Regiment (Elizabeth)
20th Infantry Regiment

Note: 183rd Infantry Division was attached for the duration of 30 November counteroffensive.

OPPOSING PLANS

THE GERMANS

Straightforward force comparisons create the impression that von Watter's under-strength Gruppe Caudry was grossly overmatched. Some accounts (including the British Official History) also observe that his three divisions in the line were deficient in artillery. This is not strictly accurate. To take the 54th Division as an example, records attest that its attached Field Artillery Regiment had 34 guns: three batteries of the versatile 10.5cm howitzer and six 7.7cm field gun batteries – a total of 34 pieces. In 1917 a German infantry division was technically allocated only three batteries of each, i.e. 24 pieces. Their problem was ammunition: just 1,500 rounds on the 54th's gun lines and a paltry reserve of 4,600. Shortfalls in hardware were much more apparent at *Gruppe* level. Von Watter's medium artillery comprised one battery of four 5.9in. howitzers and three of captured Russian, French and Belgian guns. There was also a rather incongruous detachment of coastal defence mortars. None of these weapons could range beyond 5,500m.

Strange as it might seem, the situation did not create alarm. There was unshakeable confidence in the mighty Siegfried Stellung. Having had the advantage of being designed, sited and constructed out of contact, the defences were a perfect embodiment of the latest German defensive doctrine. Termed *Eingreifentaktik* – intervention tactic – the idea was to

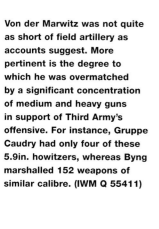

Von der Marwitz was not quite as short of field artillery as accounts suggest. More pertinent is the degree to which he was overmatched by a significant concentration of medium and heavy guns in support of Third Army's offensive. For instance, Gruppe Caudry had only four of these 5.9in. howitzers, whereas Byng marshalled 152 weapons of similar calibre. (IWM Q 55411)

The genius of German defensive planning was to be found in their use of ground. This photograph was taken from the roof of a reinforced concrete bunker on the Siegfried Stellung support line at Flesquières. It dominates the valley yet cannot be engaged until the enemy crests the far ridge. (Author's collection)

move away from heavily front-loaded linear trench systems in favour of a defence in depth. The Somme battles had proved that wire, artillery and machine guns were the key to defending ground. Large numbers of infantry had often been captured in their dugouts without making a telling contribution. These men had a much greater utility as an offensive force. Hence counterattack was the cornerstone of *Eingreifentaktik.*

Physical defences were arranged in a series of zones thousands of metres apart. The *Vorwärtszone* – 'outpost zone' – lacked traditional trench lines. Instead they built a chequerboard of mutually supporting strongpoints known as *Widerstandsnester.* These could be short sections of trench, concrete pillboxes or fortified farm buildings but they were always lightly held and bristling with machine guns. Thick belts of slanting wire would channel the enemy towards pre-planned killing areas forwards of the *Widerstand* – 'resistance line' or 'battle zone'. This contained concentric repetitions of more orthodox trench systems (known as *Stellungen*[4]) complete with telltale right-angle 'switches' and a revetted fire step. Each *Stellung* had a 'front' and 'support' trench about 200m apart, both well constructed 2.5m deep and 3.5m wide at the top. They too were studded with concrete pillboxes configured to fire in a 360-degree arc. Where possible, trenches were placed on a 'reverse slope' so that the advancing enemy would be ambushed as they crested a rise. The forward *Stellung* of the *Widerstand* was repeated by an identical support system (sometimes known as a *Zwischenstellung*) some 1,500m to the rear. Communications trenches linked them to form a thick matrix. Villages were fortified and incorporated as hubs.

With the enemy thus embroiled beyond the safety of his own lines (and supporting artillery), he would be subjected to the *Eingreifen*: counterattack by large numbers of fresh infantry with *Sturmbataillone* at their head. Planning assumptions for mounting these attacks were generous on account of the belief that the enemy's preparatory bombardment and stubborn resistance by the *Widerstand* would provide plenty of time to marshal forces.

4 Meaning literally, 'positions'.

British plans were seeking to shatter these assumptions. An intelligence report prepared in support of Operation *GY* deduced that German counterattack formations would not be in a position to influence the battle for the first 48 hours. A combination of surprise and shock action could unlock *Eingreifentaktik* before its ace card was played.

Two factors conspired to frustrate the impact of Byng's *coup de main*. By chance, the Germans were in the midst of a relief in place. On 25 November, the 20th Landwehr Division was due to be replaced in the line by 107th Infantry Division, which was redeploying from the Russian Front. Two of the 107th Division's three regiments were in the Cambrai area by 19 November, along with five of its six field artillery batteries. Secondly, some months previously the Germans had started construction of the so-called Siegfried II, an entire second *Widerstand* that ran as a backstop east of the St Quentin Canal. British accounts refer to it as the Masnières–Beaurevoir Line. Though unfinished at this stage (shallow trenches and only one belt of protective wire), it dominated the routes intended for exploitation beyond canal crossings and Bourlon Ridge. Were it not for the fortuitous presence of extra troops, only reserve battalions would have manned this line.

THE BRITISH

Third Army did not bring its entire weight to bear against Gruppe Caudry. Of six corps under command, only III and IV were to provide attacking forces to the initial thrust. Three were holding front line positions elsewhere (VII, VI and XVII) and V Corps provided the Army reserve. French High Command also offered three divisions of infantry and two of cavalry in the event of 'breakthrough'.

The task for the tanks and infantry was to penetrate the Siegfried Stellung to its full depth and secure two features: Bourlon Ridge at the north end of the breach and the crossings over the St Quentin Canal at the south. Defensive flanks would be created at both ends to secure the passage of exploitation forces. Cavalry Corps could then stream through the gap to invest Cambrai and sweep north to seize crossings over the

Bourlon Wood with the Bapaume–Cambrai road and Anneux Chapel in the foreground. Haig deemed it vital to the achievement of Operation *GY* objectives. (IWM Q 63739)

Sensée River. V Corps was ordered to advance in their wake, coming down off Bourlon Ridge and driving north to north-east. Various subsidiary attacks were scheduled across Third Army's front, as Byng wanted to create confusion about the aim and scope of his offensive.

Consistent with standard practice, initial objectives were expressed by a series of colour-coded lines like tidemarks. At first glance, this appears overly thorough – troops should be encouraged to drive deep and fast into the enemy rear areas – but it was the best means of reconciling geographic objectives with the linear creeping barrage timetables. Broadly they also corresponded with the successive belts of the Siegfried Stellung: Blue Line was the forward *Stellung* (including outpost zone), Brown Line the *Zwischenstellung* and Red Line the Masnières–Beaurevoir Line.

Lieutenant-General Sir Charles Woollcombe's IV Corps was given the northern portion of the battlefield, focusing on Bourlon Ridge. They had I Tank Brigade and 1st Cavalry Division in support. The 51st (Highland) Division sought to capture Flesquières Ridge and press east towards the spur above Cantaing as its Red Line objective, with D and E Battalions of the Tank Corps attached.[5] The Yorkshiremen of 62nd (West Riding) Division and G Battalion Tank Corps had the unenviable task of clearing Bourlon and Bourlon Wood via the village of Anneux on the Bapaume–Cambrai road. Meanwhile, 36th (Ulster) Division was to protect the flanks by attacking north up the Canal du Nord towards Moeuvres. Once the Red Line had been secured, 1st Cavalry Division was going to mount a joint attack with tanks to 'turn' Fontaine-Notre-Dame (hereafter referred to as Fontaine), Cantaing and Noyelles in succession.

III Corps had a broader frontage and more attacking divisions. With both II and III Tank Brigades in support, their main effort was the St Quentin Canal crossings at Marcoing and Masnières. The 55th (West Lancashire) Division were holding the southern 'hinge' of the battlefield from Banteux. Immediately to their north, 12th (Eastern) Division with C and F Battalions Tank Corps would advance to create a flank guard across Bonavis Ridge. The 20th (Light) Division with A and I Battalions Tank Corps aimed to capture the Blue and Brown Lines, paving the way for 29th Division's dash for the canal crossings and the

5 One company of E Battalion was cut to reinforce G Battalion.

Red Line with just one company of tanks from A Battalion. III Corps commander, Lieutenant-General Pulteney, kept 6th Division as his insurance policy, beefed up with B and H Battalions Tank Corps. It had objectives of its own through Couillet Wood but was ordered to make contingency plans for a defensive flank on the boundary with IV Corps.

He also had the headache of making space for the bulk of Kavanagh's Cavalry Corps. The 2nd and 5th Cavalry Divisions were expected to cross the canal on day one, with 4th Division planning a raid to the south-east of Cambrai towards Waincourt soon after. Each division had nearly 10,000 horses. In the opening stages of the attack, the only routes through the Siegfried Stellung would be those made by tank tracks. Horses struggled to negotiate the crushed wire so paths had to be improved by hand. They would also be in direct competition with other traffic: artillery and logistics going forwards, battle casualties and prisoners of war coming back – a staff officer's nightmare but Byng's *métier*. As proved at Vimy Ridge in April of that year, he put stock in meticulous preparation, leaving as little as possible to chance.

The first priority was his artillery. Aside from existing corps and divisional allocations, GHQ made extra weapons available. For example, four entire field artillery brigades from beyond Third Army. To this, Byng added five field artillery brigades from Third Army's central artillery train and the divisional artilleries of 40th and 56th (1st London) Divisions. All the Cavalry Corps' artillery was also pulled into the operational fire plan. In total, Byng amassed 1,003 pieces (see table for breakdown by type).

Weapon type	III Corps	IV Corps	Total
13-pdr	36	18	54
18-pdr	264	234	498
4.5in. howitzer	66	66	132
60-pdr	54	42	96
6in. gun	8	4	12
6in. howitzer	72	68	140
8in. howitzer	14	16	30
9.2in. gun	1	1	2
9.2in. howitzer	16	12	28
12in. howitzer	4	4	8
15in. howitzer	2	1	3
Totals	537	466	1,003

The lack of preparatory bombardment was both a help and a hindrance. Dispositions were made easier because there was no requirement for flash-proof cover – by the time the guns opened up, it would be too late for German counter-battery effort. Ammunition logistics was also facilitated because daily expenditures in the weeks before Operation *GY* were normal.[6] However, without the usual gradual intensification of

---

6 An absence of harassing fire would have aroused nearly as much suspicion as concerted bombardment.

effort, all the tasks associated with a preparatory bombardment (less wire crushing) would have to be achieved in a matter of hours rather than days and weeks. The situation was exacerbated by the fact that assaulting divisions expected to advance beyond the range of field artillery within hours of the offensive.

Artillery planners solved the first of these two problems by prioritizing targets and coordinating the fireplan. Headed by the obvious necessity for destruction of enemy artillery batteries, the high-priority target list went on to specify: counterattack rally points such as communication trench entrances, then command posts and finally, depth targets such as troop billets. The creeping barrage was to be dispensed with after four hours so that field guns could limber up and start pressing forwards to support the capture of depth objectives.

The Royal Flying Corps was working on its own solution to the dearth of fire support for rapid advances: fighter ground attack. Roving fighter planes could act as aerial artillery (a term still used today) to strafe and bomb enemy ground forces. They were also carving a niche for themselves conducting air interdiction well behind enemy lines, attacking enemy aerodromes, railway sidings and supply depots.

III Brigade RFC was Third Army's subordinate air wing. For Operation *GY* their six multi-role squadrons (125 aircraft) were reinforced by a further seven fighter squadrons, one reconnaissance squadron and two flights of DH4 day bombers for air interdiction missions. This brought the total up to 298. Their operation order states that tasks were to include: medium distance reconnaissance of approaches from the north, bombing of Gruppe Caudry HQ and railway junctions, ground attack of enemy forces and fighting patrols to counter enemy aircraft. Such were the perils of hurried training for low-level ground attack in the run-up to Cambrai, many pilots crashed.

Training was another of Byng's fixations. In this instance, he placed the most emphasis on tank/infantry cooperation. Opportunities for this activity were limited. Each division had just ten days to train with the tanks, which equated to two days per battalion. Fortunately, the tactics devised by Col. Fuller were simple to assimilate. Each package started

Four broad-gauge railway routes served the Cambrai build-up. In bulk terms, road-building materials took up the most space but this was followed closely by the two principal consumables: animal fodder and artillery ammunition. (IWM Q 4623)

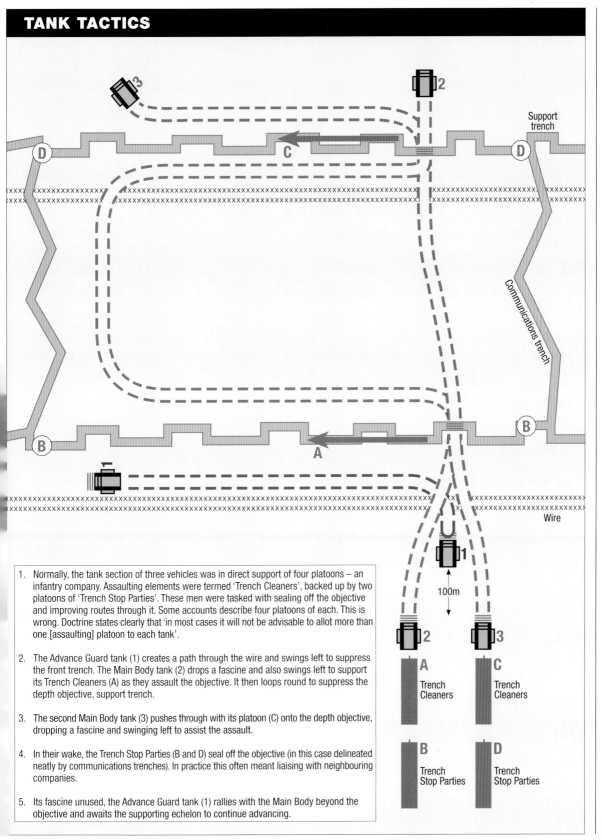

1. Normally, the tank section of three vehicles was in direct support of four platoons – an infantry company. Assaulting elements were termed 'Trench Cleaners', backed up by two platoons of 'Trench Stop Parties'. These men were tasked with sealing off the objective and improving routes through it. Some accounts describe four platoons of each. This is wrong. Doctrine states clearly that 'in most cases it will not be advisable to allot more than one [assaulting] platoon to each tank'.

2. The Advance Guard tank (1) creates a path through the wire and swings left to suppress the front trench. The Main Body tank (2) drops a fascine and also swings left to support its Trench Cleaners (A) as they assault the objective. It then loops round to suppress the depth objective, support trench.

3. The second Main Body tank (3) pushes through with its platoon (C) onto the depth objective, dropping a fascine and swinging left to assist the assault.

4. In their wake, the Trench Stop Parties (B and D) seal off the objective (in this case delineated neatly by communications trenches). In practice this often meant liaising with neighbouring companies.

5. Its fascine unused, the Advance Guard tank (1) rallies with the Main Body beyond the objective and awaits the supporting echelon to continue advancing.

A British DH4 bomber. Versatile, it also undertook reconnaissance duties and was fast enough to outdistance enemy fighters. Forward-firing Vickers and observer's Lewis machine guns provided protection. It also had dual controls, which improved survivability. Three squadrons flew at Cambrai. (IWM Q 11672)

A fascine-laden Mark IV Male manoeuvres onto railway flatcars for the journey up to Cambrai. Note how the sponson has been detached and pushed into the gunners' recess. Without this laborious adjustment they were too wide for tunnels. (Tank Museum 60/F5)

with a demonstration of the tank's capabilities in order to foster confidence. Then the platoons had a chance to practise moving behind them and working together to clear sections of trench. It was necessary to agree established drills because tanks had no satisfactory means of communicating with their accompanying infantry. All they could do was display a series of coloured discs and drop a flag to mark lanes through barbed wire.

Commonly, each infantry battalion in the lead of an advance was given a company of 12 tanks. These operated in four sections of three, the section being the basic fighting unit under command of a captain. Sections dispersed with one tank forwards (known as the 'Advanced Guard' tank) and two abreast some 100m behind. This was termed the 'Main Body'. Infantry moved in platoon 'worms' behind the main body tanks, ready to break off into trench clearance when the objective was reached.

Infantry were advised to task organize into three groupings: trench cleaners, trench stops and supports. 'Cleaners' were the fighting element while the 'stops' consolidated. 'Supports' is simply another designation for reserve, usually formed by the next echelon battalion, ready to

resume the advance onto subsequent objectives. The drill for a tank section/infantry company attack is depicted in the schematic on page 31.

Not all divisional commanders were in favour of such intimate association with tanks. Much documented is the aversion displayed by Major-General Harper, commander of the 51st Division. He felt that troops sticking too close to tanks would suffer unnecessary casualties so his infantry were forbidden to stray within 100m. Unfortunately, this was to create problems with both identifying gaps and passing through them.

Tank crews were anxious about the dimensions of the Siegfried Stellung. In the hope of creating an impassable obstacle, German engineers had built the trenches especially wide at the top. British sappers arrived at a solution reminiscent of medieval warfare. For centuries, faggots of wooden sticks known as 'fascines' had been used in siege warfare for filling in moats. Third Army ordered 400 of them to be built in three weeks. Carried above the driver's cab, fascines were deployed by dipping the tank's nose into the trench and releasing the retaining mechanism from within.

There was also concern about the inability of cavalry to negotiate crushed wire. Consequently, each tank battalion dedicated four tanks to 'wire pulling' duties. Once the assaulting battalions had passed through, these vehicles would approach the gaps and attach a sizeable four-pronged grapnel. They then dragged the torn tangles of angry barbed wire off to a flank, where it piled up like a bank of iron bramble.

Although each tank battalion already had two unarmed supply tanks (which carried fuel and ammunition for the others in its vacated sponsons), the ever-resourceful tank crews also devised long wooden sledges to ferry stores over the battlefields in advance of road building teams. The sledges came in three parts and could carry 14 tons of fuel, lubricants, ammunition, rations and water. There were 54 in total at Cambrai. Being the only vehicles large enough to carry one, each battalion also fielded a wireless tank for maintenance of contact with aircraft and/or divisional HQ.

Unsurprisingly, the wider logistic effort was equally impressive. The appetite for *matériel* betrays the true magnitude of effort in World War I. It took 36 trains to transport the 476 tanks towards the front. These were 378 fighting machines, supported by the specialist vehicles described. This tally exceeds the current total of Main Battle Tanks in the British Army (386). For the tanks alone, Third Army's light railway

network ferried forwards 750,000 litres of petrol, 34,000kg of grease, 5 million rounds of small-arms ammunition and half a million rounds of 6-pdr shells.

Road construction and improvement materials were a major consideration, not just to move combatants into position but also to ensure they could be supplied once under way. Without plank roads and teams to build them, re-supply across no man's land would have to be conducted by pack animal or porter as the sledge tanks only really took care of their own. Traffic management was a necessity, not least to prevent route degradation.

Artillery ammunition, then as now the most insatiable of all logistic demands, accounted for 5,000 tons of rail cargo. The 498 18-pdr guns stockpiled 568,000 rounds.

This hive of activity threatened to betray Byng's intentions, potentially squandering his advantage of surprise. Security therefore took precedence over all else. Planning detail was kept on as close a hold as possible, confirmation of Z-Hour not being promulgated until 18 November. All reconnaissance parties removed unit insignia.

Gun positions, supply dumps and forward assemblies of cavalry were all camouflaged. Physical preparations were controlled by dividing rear areas into zones. A belt two miles deep behind the front line was termed 'Daylight Zone'. No daylight movement was permitted in groups of over two men – even these had to remain at least 100m apart. 'Central Zone' allowed work parties but no construction as it was visible to enemy observation balloons on a clear day. Only the rear area, some five miles beyond the line, was not subject to restrictions. This procedure was aided by a period of dull, misty weather.

On 16 November, von der Marwitz reported to Rupprecht that, 'hostile attacks on a large scale against the [Second] Army front are not to be expected in the near future.'[7] The British had given no indication of an imminent offensive. All normal air and ground patrolling activity was maintained. Desultory shelling of German forward positions whistled over as usual, violating the damp tranquillity with a crump.

7 *Die Tankschlacht bei Cambrai 1917*, Reichsarchiv.

THE BATTLE OF CAMBRAI

FINAL ASSEMBLY

All the imagination and subterfuge of the preceding weeks was nearly undone by an entirely coincidental German decision to raid the front held by 36th Division on the night of 18 November. In debrief, two prisoners volunteered the information that an attack was being planned in the Havrincourt area for 20 November and tanks had been seen under nets in woodland. This came as a surprise to the Germans as a similarly successful raid against 55th Division in VII Corps area had turned up no intelligence of consequence. A report was filed to von der Marwitz, who ordered extra vigilance across Gruppe Caudry. As units arrived for the relief of the 20th Landwehr Division, he placed them under operational control of the threatened 54th Division. There was little more that he could do in so limited a time frame.

Unaware of these developments, the British pressed ahead with the process of final assembly. Under cover of darkness, artillery units had started occupying gun positions a fortnight before but the silent registration gun-line survey effort was struggling to meet this timetable. Adamant that no gun would fire spotting rounds before Z-Hour, Byng ordered the survey companies to redouble their efforts. Toiling under umbrellas and by torchlight where necessary, they managed it, 3rd Field Survey Company finishing their last task at 0200hrs on 20 November.

Royal Irish Fusiliers from 36th (Ulster) Division filing up to the front via a communications trench. Some of the infantry were in position up to 24 hours before Z-Hour. It was an uncomfortable wait.
(IWM Q 3187)

Infantry and cavalry had been called forwards as early as the night of 17/18 November, prompting an uncomfortable wait crowded into trenches, villages and woodland. Most moved on the eve of the attack. In darkness, infantry slipped and shuffled for miles along muddy roads. The pace on night moves like this always becomes uneven so the columns concertina, forcing men to march faster to catch up or wait in unexplained silence while the sweat cools on the back, bringing shivers.

Tanks waited until the last possible moment, all making their way up during the final night. Imbued with a fervent sense of occasion, Elles produced the now infamous 'Special Order No. 6' that was promulgated to all tank crews. It read:

1. Tomorrow the Tank Corps will have the chance for which it has been waiting for many months – to operate on good going in the van of the battle.
2. All that hard work and ingenuity can achieve has been done in the way of preparation.
3. It remains for unit commanders and for tank crews to complete the work by judgement and pluck in the battle itself.
4. In light of past experience I leave the good name of the Corps in great confidence in their hands.
5. I propose leading the attack in the centre division.

Tank Corps reconnaissance officers marked routes with white tape and commanders led their vehicles along it in the manner of an early motor car. In order to keep quiet, drivers were ordered to crawl forwards in second gear at a speed of under 1km per hour. 22-year-old Captain Hickey of H Battalion describes how his section was doing fine whereupon:

The tape … ended abruptly. It was quite impossible to direct the tanks by the lie of the country for the night was pitch black and no landmarks were visible. I walked ahead trying to pick out the track marks of a preceding tank by the light of a cigarette.[8]

With the forces in place by approximately 0300hrs, the men were issued their obligatory tea and rum. Crews started engines every two hours and rolled backwards and forwards to stop the tracks freezing. German captives questioned after the battle said they heard nothing of the build-up though alert sentries did detect some parties cutting preparatory lanes through British wire at about 0500hrs. This stirred up a brief but alarming artillery barrage. It seemed that the Germans knew what was coming – in retrospect J. F. C. Fuller described the sensation as 'disquieting in the extreme' – but the firing soon dissipated.

Shortly before 'the go', Elles strode along H Battalion's 27th Company, stopped at Hilda (H1), rapped it on the side with his ash stick and took his place for the advance. Across the six-mile front, crews clambered through the small hatches, sharing quips to fend off tension. Cranking handles brought the cold beasts to life with a belch of oil smoke and they sat vibrating as if in anticipation of the appointed hour.

8 *Rolling Into Action; Memoirs of a Tank Corps Section Commander*, by Captain D. E. Hickey.

A TIDE OF IRON

The tanks lurched forwards at 0610hrs precisely – ten minutes ahead of Z-Hour. Their form-up locations were half a mile or so behind the front line to minimize risk of them being heard getting into position. It also gave them a rolling start to achieve section formation.

In the blue-grey twilight, the folds of rolling countryside were blanketed in a cold pale mist; distant woods still just thin bands of black ink on the scene. In the communications trenches and sunken lanes parallel with the leisurely advance, stiff infantrymen were helping each other up, shrugging into a more comfortable fit on webbing equipment while their officers squinted to identify the allotted tank section.

Inaudible to the tank crews but heartening to any infantryman was the unmistakable, croaky whistle of passing shells. Z-Hour – 0620hrs. German front-line positions became delineated with a brilliant band of rending explosions, blast waves pulsing palpably in the damp morning air. German sentries were launching distress flares, a signal for their artillery to respond. Nothing came over in reply. British counter-battery missions were being fired from the heavier guns further back, suppressing or destroying their counterparts with remarkable precision. The regime of silent registration was vindicated, particularly as many of the Germans in front-line positions were content to remain sheltering in dugouts. They expected the bombardment to continue for some time before any assault.

The first thing to greet Advance Guard tanks was the wire. Even though the tanks had proved their wire-crushing credentials before, commanders still felt trepidation as the great swathes came into view. These belts were dense, but not impenetrable. Tanks had no difficulty forging through. In their wake, they left springy, matted beds for the infantry to negotiate, like walking on giant-sized scouring pads.

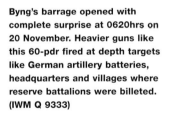

Byng's barrage opened with complete surprise at 0620hrs on 20 November. Heavier guns like this 60-pdr fired at depth targets like German artillery batteries, headquarters and villages where reserve battalions were billeted. (IWM Q 9333)

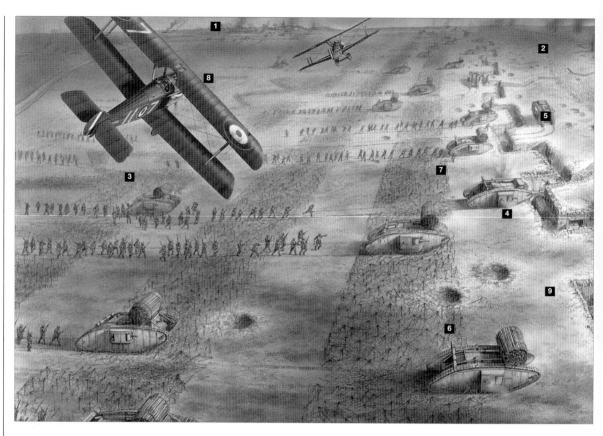

A TIDE OF IRON – THE ADVANCE OF III CORPS ON 20 NOVEMBER 1917 (pages 38–39)

36th Brigade, 12th Division, III Corps, and F Battalion Tank Corps breach the Siegfried Stellung front-line trenches south of the fortified village of La Vacquerie, 0700hrs, 20 November 1917. The concentration of tanks depicted in the field of view may appear to be exaggerated but is in fact accurate. Initial objectives in this area of the front were narrow, broadening out as 12th Division exploited towards Marcoing and Masnières. The chief concession to clarity in this illustration is the light levels. At 0700hrs on 20 November, it was still fairly gloomy and one would not have been able to distinguish La Vacquerie (1) so clearly. The protective 'creeping barrage' has now moved on to suppress the support-line defences (2), isolating forward positions for capture. Evidence of its passage forward is provided by the proliferation of fresh shell holes astride the brigade's current objective. By comparison to the Tank Tactics schematic on page 31, formations are haphazard. Ditchings or breakdowns, such as the Female Mk IV being chided by passing infantry at (3), created gaps and bunching was inevitable once the Advance Guard vehicles encountered the front line they had to cross. Dropping the fascine was complicated enough even without the presence of enemy. Poor visibility necessitated a tentative approach. The driver dipped the tank's nose into the chasm just sufficient to deploy his fascine, which filled a trench only partially (4). Rocking back with the release of this burden, he would then crawl forward, waiting for the imbalance to carry the tank into the gap as gently as possible. Applying full throttle, he would then try and claw his way out, scraping and fighting like a migrating wildebeest exiting a steep river bank. Presuming he was successful, the tank would rear up, pass its fulcrum and come crashing down on the other side, which given the absence of suspension, must have been bone jarring. Moving forward a short distance, the crew then had to negotiate a gear-crunching 90-degree turn (5). If the whole manoeuvre went wrong, the crew's only recourse was to exit the vehicle and deploy its 'unditching beam' carried on rails at the rear of the tank (6). Affixing it to the tracks with chains, the beam would be drawn underneath the tank, affording it purchase on the loose soil created by failed exits. Infantry trench-clearing platoons are keeping close to their allotted vehicle and having no difficulty negotiating the now-matted barbed wire. However, these narrow paths mean that they must wait until almost on top of the trench before being able to spread out into the assault (7). Tanks certainly gave the infantry more confidence; one passing Sopwith Camel pilot flying up the axis of advance (8) reported the glow of cigarettes on their lips. Low flight was a necessity to mitigate the threat of ground fire and passing 'friendly' artillery shells. The combination of surprise, accurate artillery fire and concentration of force has left the undermanned German infantry companies little choice but to surrender or flee (9). (Illustration by Peter Dennis)

Tanks cut paths through the vaunted wire with such ease that one commander said it may as well have been a 'bed of nettles'. Where the grapnel tanks followed, wire was piled into great banks like this one. (IWM Q 7847)

In most places, the outpost line was vanquished almost without breaking stride. Dazed defenders felt the weight of this irresistible onslaught and threw their hands up. Nevertheless, the state of terror and panic caused by the tanks is probably overemphasized. By now, many German infantrymen had seen them before. What they were not prepared for was the shock effect of an attack mounted with such surprise and momentum. Even if they did put up resistance, the tide enveloped them hopelessly quickly.

Throughout their depth, the Germans were also being subjected to ground attack by III Brigade RFC. Flying so low that one pilot recalls having to literally 'leap over' tanks, ground fire was a significant hazard, accounting for casualty rates of approximately 30 per cent per day. Even so, their contribution was telling. As planned, rear areas were harassed, artillery batteries bombed, troops and horse-drawn vehicles strafed. Pilots flew sorties all day, landing to refuel, re-arm and charge their courage with a slug of strong brandy.

In III Corps' area, 6th Division made remarkable progress. German defenders from 387th Landwehr Regiment (20th Landwehr Division) were cleared out of Couillet Wood with the assistance of snipers, cruelly analogous to driven game shooting. Either side of 6th Division, it was harder. Bolstered by retreating forces and now forewarned sufficiently to man machine guns, the support lines put up more resistance.

20th Division were pushing over Welsh Ridge and their initial objectives included the fortified hamlet of La Vacquerie. Although this fell relatively swiftly to 61st Brigade, the support lines beyond were more stubborn. Eleven tanks from A Battalion were knocked out by divisional field artillery batteries firing over open sights (a scene to be repeated elsewhere this day). The 60th Brigade to their left also became tangled in the support line. One company of the 12th/King's Royal Rifle Corps lost all of its commanders and had to be rallied by Private Albert Shepherd, an officer's runner. Similar demands were placed on the individual during the second phase of 60th Brigade's attack. A Company of 12th/The Rifle Brigade (confusingly named for an infantry regiment) faltered during their attack on a section of the support line. As per the drill, tank A2 from their accompanying section turned to

This photograph of the main street in Ribécourt was taken soon after capture – so soon in fact that German machine-gun fire damaged the camera within moments of this shot! (IWM Q 6272)

By 1800hrs on 20 November, Third Army had collected 4,211 German prisoners of war. The rate of advance at Cambrai was so great that many units surrendered simply on account of being hopelessly cut off. (IWM CO 3302)

attack but was destroyed at short range by a trench mortar. It was carrying the section commander, Captain Richard Wain, who was one of only two survivors. Dismounting a Lewis gun, he charged the troublesome position, capturing half of its garrison and routing the remainder, which he engaged with rifle fire until killed by a shot to the head. Captain Wain's posthumous Victoria Cross was the single one awarded to the Tank Corps at Cambrai.

At the southern extremity of the battlefield, 12th Division were trying to create the defensive flank against Banteux, a manoeuvre obstructed by the tenacity of isolated German positions. The 19th Reserve Infantry Regiment (9th Reserve Division) showed serious mettle in defence of four fortified farm complexes – Bleak House, Le Pavé, Pam Pam Farm and Le Quennet Farm. All had been left largely untouched by the

British bombardment, a cost of putting faith in tanks to overcome strongpoints that hitherto would have been battered by heavy artillery for days. By contrast, Bonavis Farm, which had received the attention of eight 15in. howitzer shells that morning, surrendered readily. The tanks did prove their worth and the assaulting infantry cleared the first three farms after a spirited skirmish, Pam Pam Farm being subdued by the direct fire of no less than ten vehicles. Le Quennet Farm proved tougher. The 6th/Royal West Kents (37th Brigade) even had some of their men captured. Three of the six C Battalion tanks involved were knocked out before Le Quennet's defenders saw the writing on the wall and retreated. Once Lateau Wood had been cleared, 12th Division were able to consolidate facing south-east as planned.

III Corps were doing well. Relative to recent experience, their progress was a wonder. They had trounced enemy defences that by rights should have inflicted terrible cost. By 1100hrs – in just four hours and 40 minutes – they had reached Brown Line objectives and were able to muster 55 fit tanks to lead 29th Division onto the St Quentin Canal.

HEROICS AT FLESQUIÈRES

On the northern half of the attack frontage, IV Corps were driving at Fontaine and Bourlon. Major-General Harper's 51st Division held the boundary with III Corps' 6th Division and advanced on a northerly axis towards Flesquières Ridge with the intention of exploiting onto Fontaine. His leading brigades – 152nd and 153rd – tackled the outpost and front-line systems in businesslike fashion. Those machine-gun nests that put up a fight were soon overcome by textbook platoon attacks. Map reconnaissance had created concern about a depression named 'Grand Ravine' but it proved anti-climatic. Instead, the tanks discovered that the trenches in this sector were unusually wide and deep.

Consequently, six of the 24 tanks in D Battalion (supporting 153rd) ditched. Shortly after 0900hrs the remaining tanks clambered uphill towards the railway embankment just beyond their Blue Line objective.

It was on the approach to the Brown Line beyond Flesquières that the Highlanders ran into serious trouble. This is one of the most well-known and hotly debated episodes in the battle.

Akin to the situation farther south, the support line – *Zwischenstellung* – was forewarned of the onslaught. The 27th Reserve Infantry Regiment was ordered from Marcoing to Flesquières in order to support the garrison unit, 84th Infantry Regiment. Arriving on horseback ahead of the main body, 27th Regiment's commander, Major Krebbs, was greeted by a contagious sense of confusion. Still hidden in the early morning mist, forward positions were not answering field telephones, though attack alarms and distress flares were in still in evidence. Some wounded and retreating forces began to appear with breathless and bewildered reports of innumerable tanks. Soon thereafter, the Flesquières positions came under a sharp bombardment, including smoke. The first tanks appeared. These were D and E Battalions seeking to invest Flesquières itself. Standing next to Krebbs, the 84th Regiment's commander, Major Hoffmeister, immediately was wounded in the head and evacuated. Krebbs now had overall command.

Brigade staff from 51st (Highland) Division observe the advance. 'Chateau Generalship' is the abiding impression of leadership in the Great War but by the end of 1917, 40 brigadier-generals had been killed in action or died of wounds (including one at Cambrai). (IWM Q 6326)

Two captured German MG 08/15 light machine-gunners with their Highland escort. They have not even had a chance to be relieved of their weapons so this is a timely shot. Note the wire-cutting attachment on the Highlander's Lee Enfield rifle and the canvas apron protecting his kilt. (IWM Q 6274)

The Highlanders came on. Flesquières was home to a thick concentration of field artillery, the best part of two field artillery regiments and one battery from a third. Though they had taken a pounding from British counter-battery fire and air attack by four DH5s at 0700hrs, many of the guns were still in action and had been dragged out of their emplacements into the open. This could have been done in anticipation of reported tanks but it is more likely that they were trying to stay one step ahead of the counter-battery effort. All the same, owing to the orthodox principle of reverse slope placement, they were lying in ambush.

Flesquières' *Zwischenstellung* defences were nearer the crest and they came into contact first. A furious battle flared up in and around the village. A mixed force of 600 German infantrymen was outnumbered about four to one.

A Mark IV tank destroyed by direct artillery fire. As evident from the gaping holes knocked through its steel plate, its armour offered no protection whatsoever against this threat. Worse yet, they lacked the manoeuvrability to challenge German gunnery. (IWM Q 14571)

Tanks pushed around Flesquières to outflank it and were decimated as they inched over the skyline. D Battalion lost ten tanks to the German gunners, many of whom had been specifically trained in anti-tank gunnery as part of lessons identified from the 1917 spring offensives. To the east of the village, E Battalion lost 18 – seven to 8 Battery, 108th Field Regiment alone. Unsurprisingly, the attack faltered. The systematic destruction of supporting tanks and fanaticism of Krebbs' defenders around Flesquières was making it impossible for the Highlanders to maintain a foothold. With characteristic determination, the Seaforths, Gordons and Black Watch pressed forwards repeatedly through late morning and into the afternoon. Finally, they managed to consolidate a section of trench to the south of the village and bring up machine-gun detachments to hold it.

However, the Germans had succeeded in stalling the British advance in a vitally central position. Incredulity at the failure of this attack on such a successful day has created debate. Harper's faulty tactics or the exploits of a mythical German artillery officer now identified as Unteroffizier Kruger are common explanations but commentators seem reluctant to accept that 51st Division ran into a well-trained, committed force holding perfect defensive ground. Light field guns in ambush were always going to outperform unmanoeuvrable tanks that had primitive target acquisition capabilities (a crewman peering through a narrow slit while being bounced about).

This setback had an unsettling effect on 62nd Division attacking to the north. Consistent with form of the day, the Yorkshiremen carried Blue Line objectives within a couple of hours. The only problem was Havrincourt Village, which contained a fortified chateau dominating the western extremity of Flesquières Ridge. Here the 2nd/84th Regiment put up a valiant resistance despite being bypassed and cut off very early on. G Battalion tanks had been held up at the start line trying to exit Havrincourt Wood in the dark and arrived to find the 6th/West Yorkshires pinned down in the outskirts. Direct fire from some German guns put six tanks out of action immediately but G3 made it in alone. Very

FLESQUIÈRES RIDGE AND A FOOTHOLD IN FONTAINE

20 and 21 November 1917, attack of Third Army's IV Corps

Note: Gridlines are shown at intervals of 1km/1,094yds

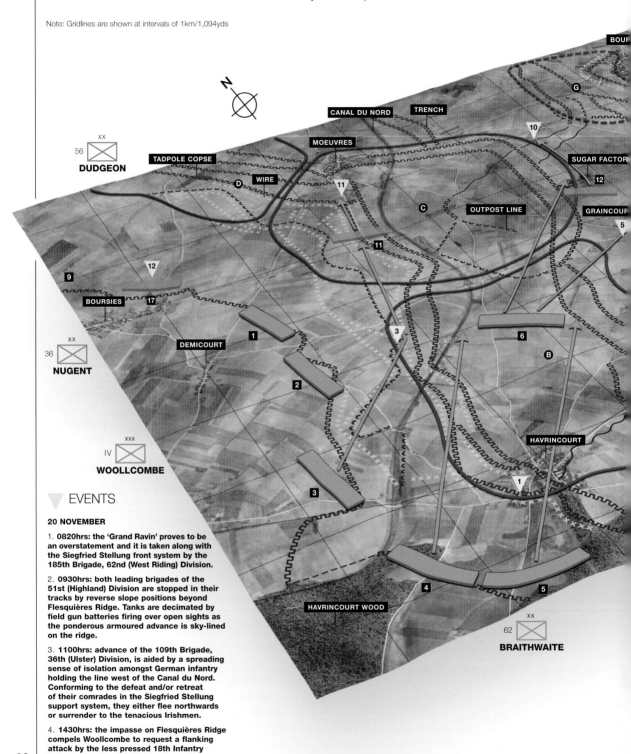

DUDGEON 56

CANAL DU NORD

TRENCH

MOEUVRES

TADPOLE COPSE

WIRE

SUGAR FACTOR

OUTPOST LINE

GRAINCOUR

BOURSIES

DEMICOURT

NUGENT 36

IV WOOLLCOMBE

HAVRINCOURT

HAVRINCOURT WOOD

BRAITHWAITE 62

BOUR

▽ EVENTS

20 NOVEMBER

1. 0820hrs: the 'Grand Ravin' proves to be an overstatement and it is taken along with the Siegfried Stellung front system by the 185th Brigade, 62nd (West Riding) Division.

2. 0930hrs: both leading brigades of the 51st (Highland) Division are stopped in their tracks by reverse slope positions beyond Flesquières Ridge. Tanks are decimated by field gun batteries firing over open sights as the ponderous armoured advance is sky-lined on the ridge.

3. 1100hrs: advance of the 109th Brigade, 36th (Ulster) Division, is aided by a spreading sense of isolation amongst German infantry holding the line west of the Canal du Nord. Conforming to the defeat and/or retreat of their comrades in the Siegfried Stellung support system, they either flee northwards or surrender to the tenacious Irishmen.

4. 1430hrs: the impasse on Flesquières Ridge compels Woollcombe to request a flanking attack by the less pressed 18th Infantry Brigade from the 6th Division towards

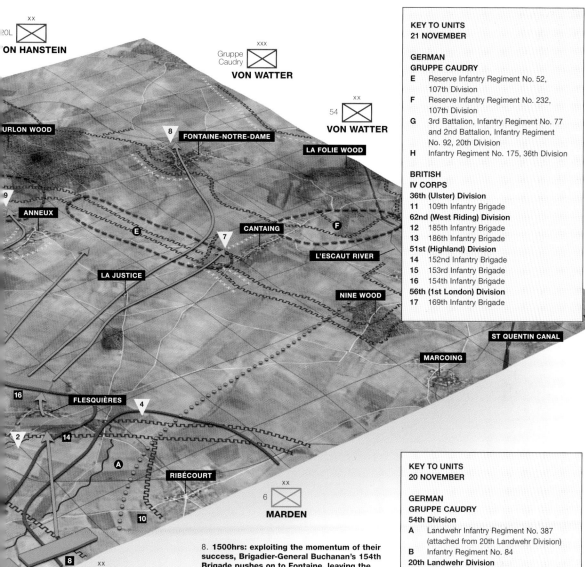

VON HANSTEIN

20L

Gruppe
Caudry
VON WATTER

54
VON WATTER

8
FONTAINE-NOTRE-DAME

LA FOLIE WOOD

URLON WOOD

ANNEUX

E

CANTAING

F

7

L'ESCAUT RIVER

LA JUSTICE

NINE WOOD

ST QUENTIN CANAL

MARCOING

16

FLESQUIÈRES

4

2

14

A

RIBÉCOURT

6
MARDEN

10

8

51
HARPER

KEY TO UNITS
21 NOVEMBER

GERMAN
GRUPPE CAUDRY

E   Reserve Infantry Regiment No. 52, 107th Division

F   Reserve Infantry Regiment No. 232, 107th Division

G   3rd Battalion, Infantry Regiment No. 77 and 2nd Battalion, Infantry Regiment No. 92, 20th Division

H   Infantry Regiment No. 175, 36th Division

BRITISH
IV CORPS
36th (Ulster) Division
11   109th Infantry Brigade
62nd (West Riding) Division
12   185th Infantry Brigade
13   186th Infantry Brigade
51st (Highland) Division
14   152nd Infantry Brigade
15   153rd Infantry Brigade
16   154th Infantry Brigade
56th (1st London) Division
17   169th Infantry Brigade

KEY TO UNITS
20 NOVEMBER

GERMAN
GRUPPE CAUDRY
54th Division
A   Landwehr Infantry Regiment No. 387 (attached from 20th Landwehr Division)
B   Infantry Regiment No. 84
20th Landwehr Division
C   Landwehr Infantry Regiment No. 384
D   Landwehr Infantry Regiment No. 386

Note: Both divisions included elements of Reserve Infantry Regiment No. 27, which was committed in full as the Gruppe Caudry operational reserve.

BRITISH
IV CORPS
36th (Ulster) Division
1   107th Infantry Brigade
2   108th Infantry Brigade
3   109th Infantry Brigade
62nd (West Riding) Division
4   187th Infantry Brigade
5   185th Infantry Brigade
6   186th Infantry Brigade
51st (Highland) Division
7   152nd Infantry Brigade
8   153rd Infantry Brigade
Flanking units
9   56th Division, IV Corps – north
10   6th Division, III Corps – south

Ribécourt. The inherent shortcomings in operational communication between corps preclude the initiative as by the time it comes to fruition, darkness is setting in.

1530hrs: despite the loss of six tanks to direct artillery fire, the village of Graincourt is captured by Brigadier-General 'Boy' Bradford's 186th Brigade at the point of the bayonet.

21 NOVEMBER

0200hrs: conforming to the defeat and/or withdrawal of units to each flank, Infantry Regiment No. 84 pulls out of Flesquières under the cover of darkness. The Highlanders of the 51st Division discover this at first light and occupy the village.

0900hrs: the 5th and 6th Seaforths of 152nd Brigade, 51st (Highland) Division, are held up on the outskirts of Cantaing by fresh reserves from the German 107th Division but the 154th Brigade pushes through with tank support.

8. **1500hrs:** exploiting the momentum of their success, Brigadier-General Buchanan's 154th Brigade pushes on to Fontaine, leaving the remnants of Cantaing's defenders to be 'mopped up' by the Seaforths. Fontaine is carried but Buchanan's men are too isolated and exhausted to consolidate properly.

9. **1300hrs:** 'Boy' Bradford's Yorkshiremen resume the push towards Bourlon and though vanquishing Anneux, attempts to capture the chapel complex on the Cambrai–Bapaume Road are frustrated by intense fire from the positions forward of Bourlon Wood.

10. **1530hrs:** the 185th Infantry Brigade, 62nd (West Riding) Division, fares better initially in its mission to roll up the Siegfried Stellung support line between Bourlon and the Canal du Nord but they too are fixed by enfilading fire from defences around Bourlon Wood.

11. The Ulsters' subsidiary operation to threaten Moeuvres and cut off its defenders from the main German positions to the east suffers from lack of tank support and thick belts of wire. Nevertheless, they succeed in getting close enough to threaten the village.

12. The 169th Brigade of the 56th (1st London) Division is stood by to attack north towards Tadpole Copse in support of the 36th (Ulster) Division but is not required.

47

With their arcs established and the guns prepared for firing, this Vickers detachment on the support line east of Ribécourt is settling down for a well-earned brew break. Consolidation of gains was a preoccupation born of hard experience. (IWM Q 6279)

Infantry doing what they do best: waiting around. Operational 'pauses' at each objective line were essential in order for the field artillery to prepare the next phase of their creeping barrage: ferrying ammunition, cooling barrels, clearing empty cases etc. (IWM Q 3177)

soon it was set ablaze by enemy fire and had to be evacuated. Its commander, 2nd Lieutenant McElroy, returned to the vehicle and killed eight Germans with his revolver before manning a Lewis gun and defending G3's wounded survivors for an hour. By then, the West Yorkshires had worked their way into the village and relieved him. Under an equally courageous Hauptmann Soltau, the remnants of 2/84th withdrew to some buildings outside the village and fought to the last man.

62nd Division went on to achieve their Brown Line objectives by 1020hrs but were starting to feel exposed on their right flank, where the Flesquières disaster was unfolding. Nonetheless, Brigadier-General 'Boy' Bradford VC – promoted at 25 years old – took up the advance with his 186th Brigade in an attempt to capture Graincourt and invest Bourlon Wood from the west. It was a tall order for just one brigade, particularly because mopping operations continued in their rear. In the event, they secured Red Line objectives in Graincourt by mid-afternoon but could go no further. Yet more field guns had taken a toll on Bradford's 13 tanks from G Battalion and he could spare only three for a tentative reconnaissance of Bourlon Wood that afternoon. Even if Bradford had been able to exploit further, 62nd Division's commander, Major-General Braithwaite, was concerned about Flesquières and ordered him to consolidate while they prepared a flanking attack. Moreover, to his left, 36th Division's subsidiary attack with 109th Brigade on the west of Canal du Nord had culminated at a similar extent.

SCRAMBLE FOR CANAL CROSSINGS

Down in III Corps, 29th Division had resumed the attack towards the St Quentin Canal, leaving forward assembly areas at approximately 1015hrs. They had been on the move since 0100hrs, covering ten miles before hitting their first objectives. Morale was high though and their push for canal crossings was joined by 59th Brigade of 20th Division to the north-west.

Planners had identified a total of ten potential crossings over the canal between Marcoing and Crèvecoeur. Beyond them lay the Siegfried II (or Masnières–Beaurevoir Line). This element of Operation *GY* was the decisive act: launching columns of marauding cavalry into German rear areas. Besides the four infantry brigades converging on these objectives, A and F Battalions of the Tank Corps managed to muster 20 and 13 tanks respectively.

Farther west, 17 tanks from H Battalion struck out for Noyelles and Nine Wood but the 71st Infantry Brigade (6th Division) that they were supporting was too concerned about the open flank with 51st Division to follow. Instead, the 6th Division infantry effort came from 16th Brigade, who were also making for Marcoing with 12 tanks from B Battalion hoping to capture the railway bridge.

As is clear from the narrative, this phase of the operation degenerated into a rather crude scramble. Formations became mixed up and tanks tended to operate somewhat independently from the infantry – especially H Battalion. Everybody was gripped by the imperative for establishing a canal bridgehead without delay. Major Phillip Hamond, commander of the F Battalion scratch force, even set off on foot to try and make sure that the Germans did not blow the bridge in Masnières.

Many eyewitnesses recall a sense of opportunity. The Germans were in full flight and the 54th Division had virtually ceased to exist. As the British infantry entered Masnières at about midday, French civilians emerged from their cellars in jubilant mood. However, German engineers succeeded in damaging the road bridge in Masnières and a withering fire from the far bank welcomed the lead elements of 88th Brigade as they approached. Snipers also populated the town, harassing the tanks and infantry as they spread out to find alternative crossings.

As much out of frustration as hope, F22 – 'Flying Fox II' – was ordered to try and negotiate the damaged bridge. In a rare moment of slapstick (as the whole crew escaped unharmed) F22 collapsed the structure, entering the water in a huge cloud of steam. Moreover, the commander

F22 'Flying Fox' photographed after the battle with some curious Germans balanced on top. It was plucky to try their luck but the resulting calamity narrowed the options for 5th Cavalry Division behind them. (Tank Museum 1546/D2)

is reputed to have lost his wig during the evacuation. 2nd/Hampshire Regiment had more success, finding a lock bridge half a mile to the east. Once across, they linked up with the two companies of 4th/Worcestershire Regiment that had already crossed on the central axis. The Newfoundland Regiment found a wooden footbridge to the west and was digging in short of Siegfried II as they had no artillery support to attack it (the assumption probably being that tanks would be across).

16th Brigade/B Battalion's advance was the first to arrive into Marcoing, seizing the railway bridge intact. 87th Brigade soon arrived to complete the town's capture. Subsequently, elements succeeded in crossing to probe Siegfried II and find Newfoundland Regiment positions west of Masnières. Two A Battalion tanks patrolled over the railway bridge and attacked Flot Farm, while 1st/Royal Inniskilling Fusiliers even assaulted and occupied a section of Siegfried II's front line. 86th Brigade arrived in Nine Wood to discover it in the hands of H Battalion's tanks, which obtained a written receipt and withdrew. Patrols from 2nd/Royal Fusiliers were thrown forwards into unoccupied Noyelles.

This rather disparate toehold on the far bank seemed adequate for cavalry at least to attempt a breakout. The Cavalry Corps had been moving forward since 0850hrs in anticipation of this so 5th Cavalry Division was in a position to release leading regiments soon after midday. Major Hamond describes the arrival of 5th Division's Canadian Cavalry Brigade in Masnières:

> Then a most ludicrous thing happened. There was a great deal of clattering, galloping and shouting and a lot of our medieval horse soldiers came charging down the street. I yelled to them that the bridge was gone but they took no notice of me and went right up to it. They turned about and came trotting back with a very piano air.[9]

Undeterred, the resourceful Fort Garry Horse made for the narrow lock bridge used by the Hampshires and managed to get B Squadron across it by 1530hrs. Unfortunately, by this stage, it was increasingly clear

The lock bridge east of Masnières in its current guise. The satchel is for scale. Even after some hasty improvement with the help of locals, it took B Squadron Fort Garry Horse half an hour to get its 150 mounts over. (Author's collection)

9 Major Hamond quoted in *The Ironclads of Cambrai*, Bryan Cooper.

to commanders on the ground that they had neither the forces nor daylight to breach Siegfried II that day. All cavalry were ordered to remain on the home bank. This message could not reach B Squadron, who had made off in the direction of Rumilly with gallant alacrity. Their commander, Captain Campbell, was killed and it fell to Lieutenant Strachan to continue. They charged an artillery battery – Strachan killing seven Germans with his sword – before making their way back in darkness. Other cavalry units already committed to the front dismounted and consolidated as infantry. For instance, 7th Dragoon Guards from 5th Cavalry Division had occupied Noyelles in that capacity.

As darkness fell on 20 November, the British held gains equating roughly to Red Line objectives. At first glance it had been a stunning success: three to four miles' penetration on a six-mile front at unprecedented speed. German reaction swung from incredulity to helpless despondency; that morning Rupprecht had considered ordering a general retirement. Cambrai was barricaded in anticipation. Even as the momentum of British attacks dissipated later in the day, the picture remained bleak. *Eingreifentaktik* failed him because the surprise and destructiveness delivered by Byng's offensive was so total. Gruppe Caudry's fighting divisions in contact had been all but wiped out; therefore forces earmarked for counterattack were now manning Siegfried II trenches. Fortuitous arrival of the relieving 107th Division plugged the most perilous gaps and six reserve battalions from neighbouring Gruppen Arras and Quentin started arriving that night. Rupprecht authorized transfer of three Army Group reserve divisions but they were still at least 48 hours away. Gruppe Caudry's situation remained highly tenuous.

Reaction in Britain was euphoric. Church bells were rung; a great victory had been achieved. Yet in the minds of the field commanders, it had fallen short of what needed to be achieved on the first day. Now surprise had been lost they would be in a race against German reserves.

B Squadron Fort Garry Horse with Lieutenant Harcus Strachan at their head. He was awarded the Victoria Cross for his gallantry and resourcefulness at Masnières. Only 23 of the squadron returned – none of them mounted. (IWM CO 2295)

No breach had been made in Siegfried II at Masnières; Flesquières had blunted the 51st Division and Bourlon Ridge was yet to be attacked. Flesquières was a frustrating failure because it held up the approach to Bourlon. It had also compelled 1st Cavalry Division to re-route south, compounding the delay in getting cavalry forwards.

Third Army's brush with unmitigated triumph invites hypothetical speculation but it is tempting to overstate the ease with which Third Army breached the Siegfried Stellung that day. Strongpoints like Havrincourt, Graincourt and Le Quennet did not fall without a fierce fight. Whilst relatively speaking, casualties had been light (approximately 4,000, some battalions not losing a single man), 179 out of 378 fighting tanks were out of action – a 47 per cent attrition rate.

It was only going to become harder. Promulgation of plans for 21 November was a priority. Byng had spoken to Haig at 1630hrs. They agreed to keep pressing without any alteration to the plan. Attempts were made to rebalance tank allocations. II Brigade (remnants of A, B and H Battalions) switched over to IV Corps. Z-Hour for III Corps around Masnières was 1100hrs. IV Corps would resume advance at 1000hrs, preceded by a preliminary dawn attack to secure Flesquières.

This looked elegant on map boards but execution was going to be problematic. Operations orders needed to cascade down to attacking battalions that were occupying forward positions. In some instances, it took hours to find commanding officers. Moreover, the men were shattered. By that evening most had been up marching and fighting for at least 24 hours. It was a foul night to be spending in the open without a hot meal: 'a dismal rain … eventually we could feel it trickling through our puttees'.[10] As the infantry curled up under groundsheets to snatch a fleeting rest, engineers, signallers and gunners toiled to improve forward lines of communication and prepare support for the resumption of attack. There was no doubting their fortitude but Third Army stood little chance of repeating the impetus of this first momentous day.

10 *Everyman at War* (1930), edited by C. B. Purdom.

It was a tedious wait for the cavalry divisions so eager to exploit. Wet, cold and bored, they gathered behind the front with only rumour and countermanded orders to break the monotony. 21 November was another day of disappointment for this group of motor machine-gunners and horse artillery. (IWM Q 6311)

A HERCULEAN REPEAT

During the night, Major Krebbs was informed that reinforcements were not forthcoming so he pulled his survivors back from the Flesquières salient to bolster defensive positions being occupied around Cantaing and Fontaine. It made good sense. They were expecting converging flank attacks to cut them off at any minute. Thus, when a reconnaissance patrol of Highlanders crept into the town under cover of darkness, they found no sign of life.

A hasty advance by 152nd and 153rd Brigades started before dawn at 0600hrs, reaching the Graincourt to Premy Chapel road (their original Red Line objective) three hours later. Contact with Germans was re-established on the outskirts of Cantaing and 154th Brigade came forwards through the drizzle to mount an attack. Tanks did not receive their orders until 0900hrs so they were late for the 1000hrs Z-Hour. Brigadier-General Buchanan pushed on without them and predictably was checked. However, this time a flanking force did arrive. Thirteen tanks from B Battalion came up from the direction of Nine Wood with the 2nd Dragoon Guards and elements of 16th Brigade; a genuine all-arms attack. Private Chris Knight was there with the Dragoons:

The village lay about three-quarters of a mile away. We galloped fiercely to the outskirts, rapidly formed sections, numbers 1 and 2 troops cantering into the village first. Donnelly, the Irishman, went raving mad, cutting and thrusting wildly at retreating Germans. Indescribable scenes followed.[11]

Cantaing was carried. Farther west, the 7th/Argyll and Sutherland Highlanders and 4th/Seaforth Highlanders (154th Brigade) took advantage of this collapse to make a dash for Fontaine in the company of six H Battalion tanks. These outstripped the infantry but were able to roam around the town creating mischief and silencing machine guns that hindered the Scottish advance. German defenders from 2nd Battalion 52nd Reserve Infantry Regiment were winkled out and fled. By nightfall, short of fuel and ammunition, the four surviving vehicles withdrew leaving the depleted Highlanders to defend the village. As the infantry consolidated in gathering gloom, troop trains could be heard pulling into Cambrai, disgorging the reinforcements they would fight the following day.

The reason these men were so isolated was that 62nd Division's thrust towards Bourlon did not make enough ground to link up. Bearing in mind that Bradford's brigade had also been in action on 20 November, they fared extremely well. His four battalions of the Duke of Wellington's Regiment bombed their way north up Siegfried Stellung support positions to invest Bourlon from the west, pushed north-east out of Graincourt to capture Anneux and even got into the quarry at the

---

11 *Everyman at War* (1930), edited by C. B. Purdom.

▼ EVENTS

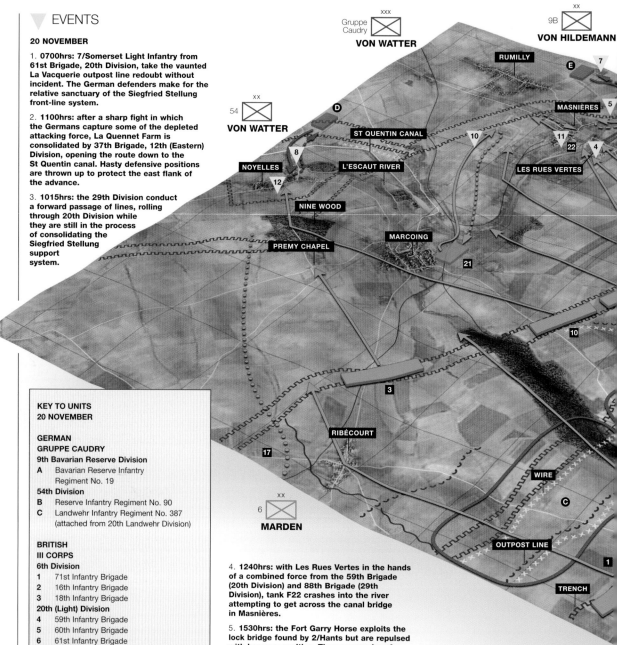

20 NOVEMBER

1. **0700hrs:** 7/Somerset Light Infantry from 61st Brigade, 20th Division, take the vaunted La Vacquerie outpost line redoubt without incident. The German defenders make for the relative sanctuary of the Siegfried Stellung front-line system.

2. **1100hrs:** after a sharp fight in which the Germans capture some of the depleted attacking force, La Quennet Farm is consolidated by 37th Brigade, 12th (Eastern) Division, opening the route down to the St Quentin canal. Hasty defensive positions are thrown up to protect the east flank of the advance.

3. **1015hrs:** the 29th Division conduct a forward passage of lines, rolling through 20th Division while they are still in the process of consolidating the Siegfried Stellung support system.

Gruppe Caudry — **VON WATTER** (xxx)

9B — **VON HILDEMANN** (xx)

RUMILLY

VON WATTER (xx) 54

ST QUENTIN CANAL

MASNIÈRES

NOYELLES

L'ESCAUT RIVER

LES RUES VERTES

NINE WOOD

MARCOING

PREMY CHAPEL

RIBÉCOURT

MARDEN (xx) 6

WIRE

OUTPOST LINE

TRENCH

**KEY TO UNITS
20 NOVEMBER**

GERMAN
GRUPPE CAUDRY
9th Bavarian Reserve Division
A   Bavarian Reserve Infantry Regiment No. 19
54th Division
B   Reserve Infantry Regiment No. 90
C   Landwehr Infantry Regiment No. 387 (attached from 20th Landwehr Division)

BRITISH
III CORPS
6th Division
1   71st Infantry Brigade
2   16th Infantry Brigade
3   18th Infantry Brigade
20th (Light) Division
4   59th Infantry Brigade
5   60th Infantry Brigade
6   61st Infantry Brigade
12th (Eastern) Division
7   36th Infantry Brigade
8   37th Infantry Brigade
9   35th Infantry Brigade
29th Division
10 86th Infantry Brigade
11 87th Infantry Brigade
88th Infantry Brigade, 29th Division in detail
12 The Newfoundland Regiment
13 1st Battalion The Essex Regiment
14 2nd Battalion The Hampshire Regiment
15 4th Battalion The Worcestershire Regiment
5th Cavalry Division
16 Fort Garry Horse, Canadian Brigade
Flanking units
17 51st Highland Division, IV Corps - North
18 55th Division, VII Corps – South

4. **1240hrs:** with Les Rues Vertes in the hands of a combined force from the 59th Brigade (20th Division) and 88th Brigade (29th Division), tank F22 crashes into the river attempting to get across the canal bridge in Masnières.

5. **1530hrs:** the Fort Garry Horse exploits the lock bridge found by 2/Hants but are repulsed with heavy casualties. The commander of the 2nd Cavalry Division (Maj. Gen. Greenly) orders his Canadian Cavalry Brigade to assist in consolidation rather than attempt further penetration as daylight is fading and no more suitable crossing sites are found.

21 NOVEMBER

6. **0630hrs:** 10/RB make an attempt to capture the lock bridge west of Crevecour but only manage to get into the village of Les Rue de Vignes. One company is left in overwatch while the remainder withdraw back towards Bonavis Ridge.

7. **1030hrs:** two German battalions make a concerted counterattack towards Mon Plaisir Farm (occupied by elements of 4/Worcesters and 2/Hants). They are met with enfilading machine guns and field artillery and driven off.

8. **1030hrs:** meanwhile, reinforcements from the 107th Division attempt to evict 2/Royal Fusiliers and 1/Lancashire Fusiliers from Noyelles. Dismounted cavalry from the 18th Hussars and 9th Lancers join the defence. Fighting continues through the day.

9. **1320hrs:** after a two-hour delay owing to absence of supporting tanks, 11/KRRC mount an attack east along the canal in order to secure crossings at Crevecour, but they come under heavy fire from the Masnières–Beaurevoir line. Four tanks assist but the force is too weak to consolidate.

10. **1400hrs:** having got 30 tanks across the Marcoing railway bridge at noon, the 87th Brigade pushes west with two battalions to link up with 88th Brigade forces in Masnières. The attack is unsuccessful owing to poor

THE LUNGE FOR CANAL CROSSINGS

20 and 21 November 1917, attack of Third Army's III Corps

Note: Gridlines are shown at intervals of 1km/1,094yds

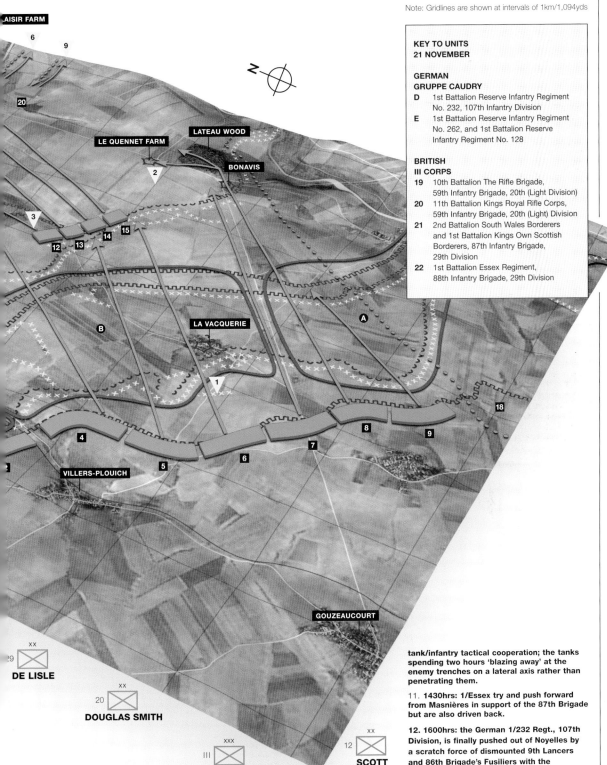

**KEY TO UNITS
21 NOVEMBER**

**GERMAN
GRUPPE CAUDRY**

D 1st Battalion Reserve Infantry Regiment
No. 232, 107th Infantry Division
E 1st Battalion Reserve Infantry Regiment
No. 262, and 1st Battalion Reserve
Infantry Regiment No. 128

**BRITISH
III CORPS**

19 10th Battalion The Rifle Brigade,
59th Infantry Brigade, 20th (Light Division)
20 11th Battalion Kings Royal Rifle Corps,
59th Infantry Brigade, 20th (Light) Division
21 2nd Battalion South Wales Borderers
and 1st Battalion Kings Own Scottish
Borderers, 87th Infantry Brigade,
29th Division
22 1st Battalion Essex Regiment,
88th Infantry Brigade, 29th Division

AISIR FARM

LE QUENNET FARM

LATEAU WOOD

BONAVIS

LA VACQUERIE

VILLERS-PLOUICH

GOUZEAUCOURT

DE LISLE

DOUGLAS SMITH

PULTENEY

SCOTT

tank/infantry tactical cooperation; the tanks
spending two hours 'blazing away' at the
enemy trenches on a lateral axis rather than
penetrating them.

11. **1430hrs:** 1/Essex try and push forward
from Masnières in support of the 87th Brigade
but are also driven back.

12. **1600hrs:** the German 1/232 Regt., 107th
Division, is finally pushed out of Noyelles by
a scratch force of dismounted 9th Lancers
and 86th Brigade's Fusiliers with the
assistance of two tanks.

southern tip of Bourlon Wood before being forced to retire. As the British Official History attests, 186th Brigade had accomplished tasks that 'would have taxed a fresh division'.[12] After dark they were relieved by 185th Brigade, which held a line along the Cambrai–Bapaume road up to Anneux Chapel.

It was an altogether more chaotic day for III Corps, principally on account of German aggression. The Hampshires and Worcestershires had spent the night street fighting in Masnières and their haggard faces greeted the dawn 200m beyond the town towards Rumilly. 10th/The Rifle Brigade mounted an operation at 0630hrs to force a canal crossing at a lock bridge south of Crèvecoeur. It proved impossible as overlapping machine-gun arcs swept the gates. More disruption was delivered by 1st/232nd Reserve Infantry Regiment's concerted counterattack against Noyelles at 1030hrs. An eclectic band of defenders from the Lancashire Fusiliers, Royal Fusiliers and 18th Hussars were joined by one dismounted squadron of 9th Lancers and two tanks from B Battalion to keep the attackers at bay. Other elements of 86th Brigade were also in action all day trying to keep Germans out of Nine Wood.

The St Quentin Canal valley echoed with a persistent stutter of machine-gun fire that grey November morning as 87th Brigade postured to throw itself at Siegfried II between Noyelles and Marcoing. Joined by 17 tanks from A and F Battalion, this operation never achieved any momentum. With only one crossing, the force trickled into action achieving no breach for the two battalions of infantry to exploit. Whilst only three tanks were actually knocked out, surviving vehicles limped back in a sorry state. German reinforcements in this sector had been issued with armour-piercing ammunition. A54 returned with 100 holes in it.

The 59th Brigade's similar effort to the east of Masnières proved equally inconclusive. Its four supporting F Battalion tanks failed to arrive until 1500hrs – 90 minutes into the battle. They found 11th/King's Royal Rifle Corps huddled on the home bank in a furious firefight having only got one company across the canal. Cognisant of F22's fate, tank crews expressed understandable reluctance to cross the wooden bridge so they cruised up and down the bank adding little value to proceedings.

Pulteney's efforts to get III Corps through Siegfried II were fast entering the realm of folly. The 88th Brigade never even crossed the start line on their attack. The men were too exhausted. At the same time as their divisional commander, Major-General de Lisle, reported this, Pulteney was already in discussion with Third Army about ceasing offensive operations altogether. There was no decision to make.

That evening, Byng and Haig discussed the situation. 48 hours had always been the desired period to assess the merit of persisting with Operation GY. Further attacks on the St Quentin Canal were out of the question. Discussion rested on whether to persevere with Bourlon. V Corps' three divisions of infantry were available and the alternative was a general retirement back to the vicinity of Brown Line objectives. If they could seize Bourlon Ridge, it would form the basis of a solid

12 British Official History, *The Battle of Cambrai 1917*, Captain Wilfrid Miles.

consolidation of what had already been achieved. At this stage, Anneux, Fontaine and Cantaing were in British hands. Haig opted to proceed.

The problem was that the operation would require deliberate preparation, taking time that favoured a German force frantically reinforcing. Haig compromised by selecting 23 November, leaving one day for what he termed, 'housekeeping'.

'HELL'S LADIES' DANCE IN FONTAINE

Fontaine's defenders were not given that breather. In a bid to link up, 7th/Argyll and Sutherland Highlanders were withdrawn during the night and placed below Bourlon Wood east of Anneux. Four companies of Seaforth Highlanders remained and spread themselves to cover the 3,500m perimeter. Enemy aircraft were spotted in the ubiquitous dawn drizzle; artillery fire shrieked in soon thereafter. Gruppe Caudry used recent arrivals from 119th Infantry Division to assault Fontaine – 1st and 2nd/46th Regiment. At 1000hrs, they attacked under a barrage from the south-east, utilizing machine guns in La Folie Wood. Distress rockets begged assistance from 51st Division's field artillery but they were lost in the mist. The Seaforths were alone. For six hours, the streets of Fontaine rang with the cacophony of battle. Although already low on ammunition, the kilted Scotsmen lived up to their German moniker 'Hell's Ladies' in Fontaine. Many outposts fought to the death. Wild, screaming counterattacks sprang from side streets before the German infantry could establish themselves at junctions. When cornered by six Germans and bid to surrender, the wounded commanding officer, Lieutenant-Colonel Unthank, sprang up and escaped by clubbing them with his empty rifle. For all this, the outcome was never in doubt and Unthank led the beleaguered remnants of his battalion back to Cantaing at 1430hrs, leaving 319 men behind.

The 62nd Division also bore the weight of counterattack on their day off. All three West Yorkshire Regiment battalions of 185th Brigade were attacked soon after 0700hrs. Augmented by strafing runs from low-flying aircraft, both gas and high-explosive shells rained down on the shallow trenches they had prepared overnight, clearing the way for a fast-moving infantry assault by mixed elements of 386th Landwehr Regiment and the newly arrived 50th Regiment. Akin to their tenacious colleagues at

On the morning of 22 November, Lt. Col. Unthank centred his battalion's defence of Fontaine on this now derelict railway station. Their unequal struggle encapsulates the doggedness of 51st Division at Cambrai. (Author's collection)

Fontaine, the Yorkshiremen put up a forceful resistance, answering the inevitable retirement with counterattacks in spite of high casualties amongst officers. Collapse was averted by the afternoon but gains made on 21 November were largely effaced.

The 36th Division and 56th Division launched the only British attacks of the day, continuing the effort to capture Moeuvres. The 12th/Royal Inniskilling Fusiliers were pushed back to their start lines but the London Scottish of 56th Division took Tadpole Copse to the west. Woollcombe's proactivity also included the night-time relief of 62nd Division by 40th Division; an activity necessitated by the steady accumulation of casualties sustained in the previous three days.

The attack frontage for 23 November was almost as large as the original push had been: just short of six miles. IV Corps amassed an impressive array of artillery pieces to support the operation: 40th Division had six field artillery brigades under command. For his part, Elles cajoled and cannibalized 88 tanks into action, rearranging orders of battle, crews and commanders as necessary. Fifty RFC fighters would operate in direct support of ground operations and keep German aircraft at bay.

In outline, the plan was simple. The 51st Division would have another go at Fontaine with 152nd Brigade. At first glance, it appears to be rather a modest force that Harper put into action but the Highlanders were embarking upon their fourth day of continuous action. Some battalions were down to less than 100 effective combatants. Thirty-six tanks from B, H and C Battalions would accompany them, with a further 11 from I Battalion lying in wait alongside Harper's composite reserve of six companies.

40th Division had their sights on Bourlon Ridge. 29 tanks from G and D Battalions were mustered to support Major-General Ponsonby's two attacking brigades: the Welsh 119th attacking Bourlon Wood and 121st, Bourlon village. Protecting their left flank was 36th Division with its daily attempt at driving the Germans from Moeuvres. This time it was the turn of 108th Brigade but now with 11 E Battalion tanks in support. Buoyed by their successes the previous day, 56th Division were also in the fray, exploiting farther north-west up the Siegfried Stellung from Tadpole Copse.

Opposing them was Gruppe Arras under the command of Generalleutnant von Moser. He had two divisions in the line opposite this offensive – 20th in Moeuvres and Inchy and 214th around Bourlon. He kept 21st Division in reserve and could expect the services of 3rd Guards Division when they had detrained from Flanders. Gruppe Caudry still controlled the front at Fontaine and Cantaing, with the disjointed 107th Division now bringing 119th Division regiments under command.

'A TOT OF RUM AND WE WERE OFF'

On yet another cold, wet and windy day, the 6th/Gordon Highlanders formed up once more, hoisting Lewis guns onto their shoulders and fixing bayonets. Their 19 tanks ambled noisily into position while the shells made shrill passage overhead. Once under way, the absence of smoke exposed them to a withering barrage of machine-gun fire from the east. German Maxim gunners sent streams of tracer arcing towards the distant blobs of encumbered men marching into Fontaine. As the Gordons neared the town, the creeping barrage lifted, allowing more German weapons to range in. They were halted 400m short of the objective and went to ground. Impervious to this deadly rain, the tanks forged ahead. Feeling naked and taking casualties, a few infantrymen probably felt a bit jealous. Given the fate that awaited these crews, they needn't have. Only six were destined to return.

On approach, the going was good; German outpost pickets being mown down as they fled. However, once inside Fontaine, their fortunes reversed. A battery of lorry-mounted K.Flak anti-aircraft guns lay in wait. Two of them together accounted for seven tanks.

> Soon, as into a rat trap, came nine tanks in procession towards Fontaine. The gun crews stood to their guns, burning with eagerness. [Hauptman Haehner] commanded: 'Steady men, it will soon be time'. When the tanks were hardly 100m away, the command rings: 'Rapid fire!' The first tank rears upwards.[13]

Four other B Battalion vehicles suffered an incredible intensity of small-arms fire and audacious assaults from German infantry with bundled hand grenades, nicknamed 'ball charges'. Only three tanks from B Battalion's force made it back to the start point. The six-strong C Battalion force fared a little better, principally because they did not encounter the K.Flak battery. Still, two were knocked out by infantry in the village and one broke down.

Harper's left axis was directed at the area between Fontaine and Bourlon Wood, with 6th/Seaforth Highlanders and 15 tanks from C and H Battalion. Untroubled by the enfilade fire from La Folie Wood (they were beyond range), the Seaforths achieved their objectives, fashioning a loose outpost line to the north-west of Fontaine. C Battalion's tank section sniffed their way into Bourlon Wood looking for trouble. One became bogged but the other two fought alongside 40th Division. H Battalion's company focused on trying to create a break into Fontaine

---

13 Anonymous German eyewitness quoted in *Following the Tanks*, Jean-Luc Gibot and Philippe Gorczynski.

A pair of motorized K.Flak Batterie anti-aircraft guns. In a chilling foretaste of the infamous 88mm's potency during World War II, these flak guns proved highly effective in the direct fire anti-tank role, accounting for at least 64 Mark IVs during the course of the battle.
(IWM Q 44156)

With a macabre likeness to an incinerator, the hatches on this Mark IV reveal its immolated crew. They had precious little time to extract themselves once the volatile mix of fuel, motor oil and ammunition ignited. (Tank Museum 1546/D4)

for the Seaforths. Six vehicles fought along the north-eastern outskirts all day, some Scotsmen perching on their backs. Ultimately, the defences were too thick.

The failure of these attacks was deeply frustrating for the 51st and illustrates one of the inherent shortcomings of fledgling tank warfare. In the linear context of 20 November, protected by creeping barrage and applying rehearsed drills with overwhelming concentrations, it all came together. Deviate from that template and prevailing truths were exposed. Unless tackling a lone strongpoint head on, tanks provided no *physical* protection for infantry. At Fontaine, they attacked a multi-faceted position from a kilometre's distance at the speed of a walk. The enfilading machine guns of La Folie and Bourlon Wood were able to fire as if the tanks were not there. Once inside a built-up area, the limitations of armour are self-evident. When all is said and done, the attacking force lacked manoeuvre and, in the absence of that, artillery is the vital factor. Therefore, it will come as no surprise to discover that of all the divisions in action on 23 November, the 51st had the lowest allocation of heavy artillery.

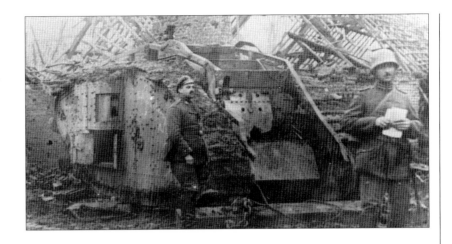

BOURLON BLOODED

Bourlon Wood is really more like a forest – a dense mix of deciduous and evergreen trees dissected by long rides and sunken roads. Dips, gullies and mounds interrupt the general uphill trend until you emerge on the far side and look down into Bourlon itself, snuggled up against the shoulder of the ridge. By 23 November, both were infested with machine-gun nests, dugouts and barricades. Preparatory shelling of the wood had commenced the day before, adding explosive and pine sap to the cloying aroma of decaying leaves. Shattered boughs littered the already profuse undergrowth.

This dark, foreboding mass cast a sort of shadow on the Welshmen of 119th Brigade as they filed into position to attack. It felt colder than usual. Sixteen tanks from G Battalion were late so a section of D Battalion was switched over from the neighbouring 121st Brigade. They clattered into position, the crews by now complete veterans. The 40th Division had never worked with them before but it was simple enough: 'follow our lead and keep close'.

No sooner had the infantry advanced, they were in disarray. On the right, 19th/Royal Welch Fusiliers felt compelled to pause in the old quarry and reorganize. The 12th/South Wales Borderers were struggling up on the left. Major Watson of D Battalion recalls the scene:

> On the hillside on the left we could mark the course of the battle – the tanks with tiny flashes darting from their flanks – clumps of infantry following in little rushes – an officer running in front of his men until suddenly he crumpled up and fell, as though some unseen hammer had struck him on the head … the wounded staggering painfully down the hill.[14]

Two hours later, somehow this ragged passage had reached the north end of the wood and the intermingled survivors prepared a loose defensive line. Counterattack was inevitable. Brigadier-General Crozier split the reserve battalion (17th/Welsh Regiment) in two and sent them forwards to stiffen his slender grip on the ridge. G Battalion tanks had arrived by now as well.

---

14 *A Company of Tanks*, Major W. H. L. Watson.

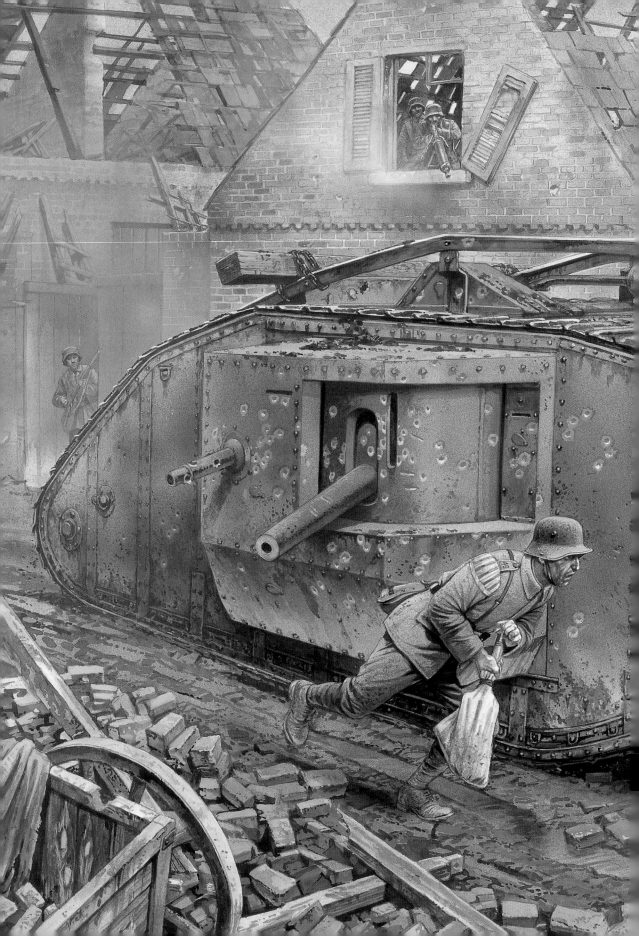

THE CRIPPLING OF 'BANDIT II' – FONTAINE,
23 NOVEMBER 1917 (pages 62–63)

Mark IV tank B23 from B Battalion Tank Corps being attacked by Germans from the 2nd Battalion, 46th Infantry Regiment (119th Infantry Division), in Fontaine, 1100hrs, 23 November 1917. B23 had become separated from the main force on entering the village and was preyed upon by a company of German infantry under command of a Leutnant Spremberg. His testimony has survived. Having failed to subdue the 'roaring lion' with single hand grenades (1), he 'ordered empty sandbags to be brought and four hand grenades be placed in them, with one grenade tied near the top of the bag' (2). Concentrating fire on the vision slits to occupy the vehicle (3), Musicians Buttenberg and Schroeder – both trained *Stosstruppen* – rushed forward and tossed their charges under B23's left-hand track (4). The resulting explosion tore the track clean off the vehicle but Spremberg's men were unable to finish it off because the survivors kept up a withering fire until rescued by a second unidentified Mark IV.

The fighting conditions experienced by tank crews in Fontaine that day are exemplified by the testimony of Captain Groves, commander of Number 1 Section, B Battalion. He was riding in a Male tank, B19. 'Hell was let loose as we turned into the street. We were being fired at from the roofs – front, back and sides. A combination of splash and armour flaking [spall] made it most difficult to see anything when handling a gun … The gun ports were all lit up with sparks.'

This had the effect of 'shot-blasting' the armour plate and often damaged the cooling sleeves around the Lewis gun barrels (5).

'Imagine the shouting required to get the [6-Pounder] guns onto the machine guns in the houses. Whenever I spotted a target I had to yell instructions in the driver's ear, then dash over to the other side of the tank to the 6-Pounder gunner, pinch or punch him to attract his attention and bawl into his ear where the target was … The atmosphere at this time was warming up, what with the engine fumes and fumes from 6-Pounder backflash. There were two men wounded and all the crew's faces were covered with blood … Then, as I was observing with the periscope through the roof, I was pinched violently in the leg, looked round and saw the tank was on fire at the back of the batteries. I pointed to the door to Sgt Stewart and he stood by with his hand ready to open it. I can honestly say at this moment I thought "Death by fire or bullets, well, bullets for my own choice". The bullets were banging on the door like large hailstones on plate glass.' Captain Groves managed to put the fire out with three extinguishers and direct the vehicle out of Fontaine to safety. He was fortunate. Fire most often raged with terrifying speed and intensity once initiated, creating a feral and often futile scramble for inaccessible hatches. (Illustration by Peter Dennis)

West of the wood, 121st Brigade was forging forwards towards Bourlon. Their fortunes were slaved in part to 36th Division's attack up the Siegfried Stellung support line east of the Canal du Nord, which had not gone well. Attacking parallel to the trenches, seven out of 11 tanks had been knocked out and the Ulstermen faltered, meaning that German machine guns were able to enfilade 13th/Green Howards on the extreme left of 40th Division's advance. 20th/Middlesex Regiment was just beyond their reach and managed to storm the south corner of the village with seven of D Battalion's tanks making it in with them. They lacked the numbers to exploit the opening and three tanks were destroyed almost immediately. 21st/Middlesex attempted to push forwards in support but suffered grievously at the hands of German artillery, now finding its range on this obvious approach route.

At 1500hrs, German infantry from 175th Regiment and 9th Grenadier Regiment organized themselves to counterattack the wood. Under a lightning barrage, their determined rush bowled the Welshmen back to a sunken road where they rallied, surging through the trees to regain the ridge, berserk with rage. The wood witnessed a chaotic savagery. Amidst a pounding artillery duel that assailed all the senses, visibility was minimal. Dodging and charging forwards over bodies ripped open by shrapnel, the Welshmen closed with their opponents, firing, clubbing and shoving their way forwards. Command and control had evaporated long ago. Handfuls of men decided the outcome. Immune to the feeble entreaties of wounded enemy, acts of pitiless murder stand equal to conspicuous gallantry in such situations. All the certainties of right and wrong have no voice. The only communicable language is violence.

Imagine then the Welshmen's breathless recovery as the Grenadiers' survivors fled down towards Bourlon, a few being sought out by bursts of machine-gun fire. Shaking, numbed, relieved; hardened non-commissioned officers already barking commands to reorganize.

The senior commander left alive was Lieutenant-Colonel Plunkett, commanding officer of 19th/Royal Welch Fusiliers. He established his brigade headquarters in a hunting lodge and waited for further reinforcement. It was not long in coming. As evening arrived, 120th Brigade was fed into the front piecemeal.

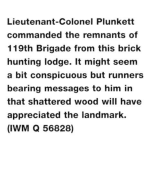

Lieutenant-Colonel Plunkett commanded the remnants of 119th Brigade from this brick hunting lodge. It might seem a bit conspicuous but runners bearing messages to him in that shattered wood will have appreciated the landmark. (IWM Q 56828)

▼ EVENTS

23 NOVEMBER

1. **1030hrs:** 6/Gordons' infantry cannot find a way thorough the tough outer defences of Fontaine. Later attempts by 152nd Brigade reserve also falter. They are forced to dig in an outpost line 500m short of the town.

2. **1130hrs:** The supporting tanks of B and C Battalion get into the village but are decimated by direct fire from K.Flak Batterie 7 and infantry rushes with bundled grenades. Only three of B Battalion's 13 tanks make it back.

3. **1200hrs:** Royal Welch Fusiliers on the right flank of 119th Brigade's attack into Bourlon Wood fare well initially, reaching the northern extremity after a hard fight through the wood.

4. **1500hrs:** concerted counterattacks by the fresh troops from Grenadier Regiment No. 9 and Infantry Regiment No. 175 drive the centre of 40th Division's attack back towards the sunken road. With Germans infiltrating to their rear, the Fusiliers and Seaforths on the east of the wood are compelled to conform. Both Battalions of the Welsh Regiment are pushed into the line.

5. **1700hrs:** exposed to their west flank and pressed hard by local counterattacks, there is no chance of the Green Howards and Middlesex on the left of 40th Division capturing Bourlon as tasked so they withdraw to a hasty outpost line on the spur to the south.

24 NOVEMBER

6. **0001hrs:** through the night, the indefatigable Lt. Col. Plunkett's 119th Brigade are reinforced by composite elements of 120th Brigade's infantry battalions and dismounted cavalry. The Germans also reinforce their positions with Guards Fusilier Regiment, 3rd Guards Division, and the remaining two battalions of Reserve Infantry Regiment No. 46.

7. **1530hrs:** 14th Battalion Highland Light Infantry, is launched at Bourlon with 12 tanks in support. Whereas the tanks are compelled to withdraw by withering close range fire from armour-piercing ammunition, the Glaswegians of the HLI bypass the town centre and reach the north-east corner relatively unscathed.

8. **1600hrs:** meanwhile, the Germans counterattack in Bourlon Wood with now characteristic fury. This precludes any British advance, thus leaving the Highland Light Infantry isolated in Bourlon. A subsidiary attack by the Suffolks to the north-west of Bourlon also fails.

9. **2130hrs:** an exhausted and depleted 51st (Highland) Division is relieved by the newly arrived 1st Guards Brigade from the Guards Division in Army reserve. 2nd Battalion, Scots Guards (from 3rd Guards Brigade), is sent into Bourlon Wood to shore up the right side of 119th Brigade.

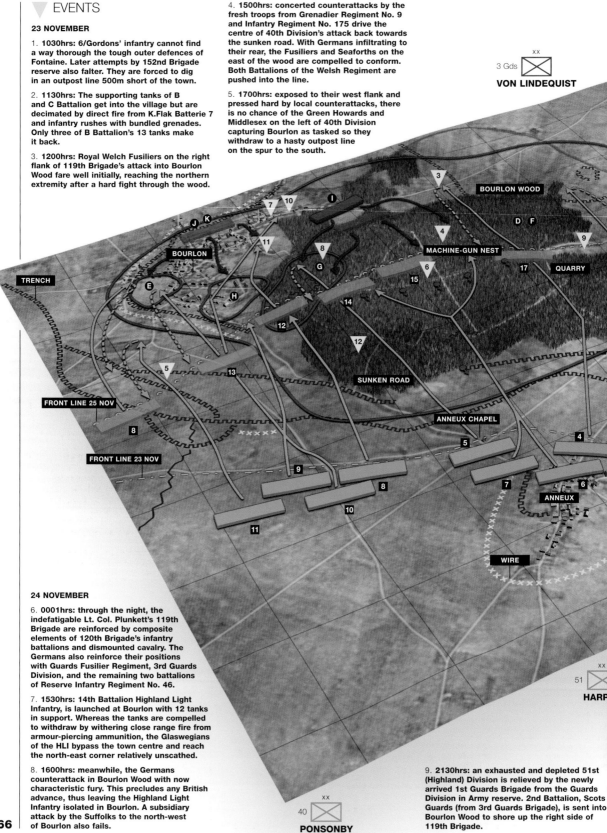

3 Gds
VON LINDEQUIST

BOURLON WOOD

MACHINE-GUN NEST

QUARRY

BOURLON

TRENCH

SUNKEN ROAD

ANNEUX CHAPEL

FRONT LINE 25 NOV

FRONT LINE 23 NOV

ANNEUX

WIRE

51
HARP

40
PONSONBY

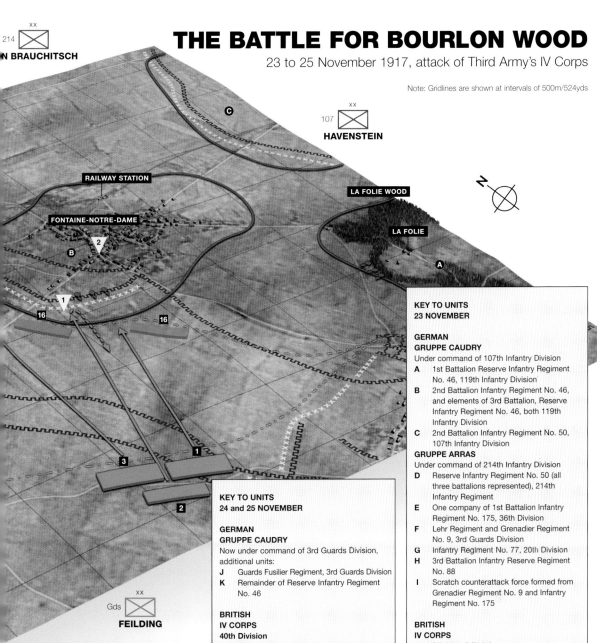

THE BATTLE FOR BOURLON WOOD
23 to 25 November 1917, attack of Third Army's IV Corps

Note: Gridlines are shown at intervals of 500m/524yds

214 [XX] BRAUCHITSCH

107 [XX] HAVENSTEIN

C

RAILWAY STATION

LA FOLIE WOOD

FONTAINE-NOTRE-DAME

LA FOLIE

B   2

A

1

16   16

3   1

2

Gds [XX] FEILDING

KEY TO UNITS
23 NOVEMBER

GERMAN
GRUPPE CAUDRY
Under command of 107th Infantry Division
A   1st Battalion Reserve Infantry Regiment
     No. 46, 119th Infantry Division
B   2nd Battalion Infantry Regiment No. 46,
     and elements of 3rd Battalion, Reserve
     Infantry Regiment No. 46, both 119th
     Infantry Division
C   2nd Battalion Infantry Regiment No. 50,
     107th Infantry Division
GRUPPE ARRAS
Under command of 214th Infantry Division
D   Reserve Infantry Regiment No. 50 (all
     three battalions represented), 214th
     Infantry Regiment
E   One company of 1st Battalion Infantry
     Regiment No. 175, 36th Division
F   Lehr Regiment and Grenadier Regiment
     No. 9, 3rd Guards Division
G   Infantry Regiment No. 77, 20th Division
H   3rd Battalion Infantry Reserve Regiment
     No. 88
I   Scratch counterattack force formed from
     Grenadier Regiment No. 9 and Infantry
     Regiment No. 175

BRITISH
IV CORPS
51st (Highland) Division
152th Infantry Brigade – Brigadier-General Burn
1   6th Battalion Seaforth Highlanders
2   6th Battalion Gordon Highlanders
3   Mixed force from 5th Battalion Seaforth
     Highlanders and 8th Battalion Argyll and
     Sutherland Highlanders
40th Division
119th Brigade – Brigadier-General Crozier
4   19th Battalion Royal Welch Fusiliers
5   12th Battalion South Wales Borderers
6   17th Battalion Welsh Regiment
7   18th Battalion Welsh Regiment
121st Brigade – Brigadier-General Campbell
8   12th Battalion Suffolk Regiment
9   20th Battalion Middlesex Regiment
29th Division
10   13th Battalion Green Howards
11   21st Battalion Middlesex Regiment

KEY TO UNITS
24 and 25 NOVEMBER

GERMAN
GRUPPE CAUDRY
Now under command of 3rd Guards Division,
additional units:
J   Guards Fusilier Regiment, 3rd Guards Division
K   Remainder of Reserve Infantry Regiment
     No. 46

BRITISH
IV CORPS
40th Division
120th Brigade – Brigadier-General Willoughby
12   13th Battalion East Surrey Regiment
13   14th Battalion Highland Light Infantry
14   11th King's Own (Royal Lancashire
     Regiment) and balance of 14th Battalion
     Argyll and Sutherland Highlanders
15   9th Cavalry Battalion (15th Hussars, 19th
     Hussars and 1st Bedfordshire Yeomanry)
     in dismounted role
Guards Division
*1st Guards Brigade – Brigadier-General
Champion de Crespigny*
16   2nd Battalion Grenadier Guards,
     2nd Battalion Coldstream Guards,
     3rd Battalion Coldstream Guards,
     1st Battalion Irish Guards
*3rd Guards Brigade – Brigadier-General Lord
Seymour*
17   2nd Battalion Scots Guards

25 NOVEMBER

10. **0615hrs: 13th Battalion East Surreys,
mount a link-up operation into Bourlon in
a bid to relieve the Highland Light Infantry.
Despite attacking without tanks (they were
late), the East Surreys reach Battalion HQ
near the church. They are unable to get any
further towards the main body at the north
end of the town.**

11. **0930hrs: Having withstood 16 hours of
onslaught without support of any kind, the
three companies of Highland Light Infantry
holed up around the railway station in Bourlon
are forced to surrender. Only 80 men survive.**

12. **1730hrs: 186th and 187th Brigades from
62nd (West Riding) Division conduct relief in
place with the beleaguered survivors of 119th,
120th and 121st Brigades on the Bourlon
front. The 13th East Surreys remains at the
southern end of Bourlon until 27 November.**

56th Division's operation to expand their gains beyond Tadpole Copse made a degree of progress towards Inchy and the 36th Division operation west of the Canal du Nord had managed once again to penetrate Moeuvres. Regrettably for both enterprises, problems east of the canal and around Bourlon village made it difficult to press further. Besides, Gruppe Arras was not ready to give up Moeuvres. The 108th Brigade's tenancy there was as short-lived as ever; 2nd/88th Reserve Regiment delivering a counterattack that forced the Ulstermen to withdraw to the outskirts after dark.

For now, the whole focus of the offensive switched to 40th Division around Bourlon. Byng brought the Guards Division under Woollcombe's command and they promptly relieved 51st Division on the Cantaing–Fontaine front – not before time. In addition, he authorized the formation of two dismounted cavalry battalions (Bedfordshire Yeomanry and 19th Hussars) to bolster 121st Brigade. Plans for 24 November put the balance of 120th Brigade into that attack against Bourlon. 14th/Highland Light Infantry and 12th/Suffolks would strike the village with 12 tanks from I Battalion; essentially the last serviceable vehicles left in Third Army. 13th/East Surreys were to come down off the ridge and envelop Bourlon from the north-east. Logistic constraints (artillery ammunition and tank refit) meant that Z-Hour could not be arranged before 1500hrs.

DAS RINGEN UM BOURLON

For the first time since 20 November, von Moser could bolster his miscellaneous collection of defenders at Bourlon with a substantial injection of reserves. The 3rd Guards Division arrived in the Bourlon sector on 23 November with its Lehr, 9th Grenadier and Guard Fusilier Regiments; units going straight into action as the situation demanded. The *Gruppe* system was much in evidence, with the commander of the incumbent 50th Regiment remaining in charge despite his men being a minority.

Rupprecht and von der Marwitz were still engaged in damage limitation. Large-scale, deliberate counterattack was not an option until at least 27 November. That did nothing to diminish the offensive spirit of local commanders and the defenders of Bourlon took every opportunity. In command of 9th Grenadier Regiment was Colonel von

North-east Bourlon changed hands constantly during the six days it was fought over. Three years on, these trees still show evidence of shell damage. (IWM Q 37254)

Pacsynksi. In the early hours, he paraded a scratch force of able-bodied *Feld Grau* (infantry) and led them into a dawn attack against Plunkett's positions in the north-east corner of the wood.

On the approach, Feldwebel-Leutnant Hohenstein's platoon captured a two-man British listening post, which betrayed the exact location of 119th Brigade's forward positions as 50 yards farther into the wood. Fanning out noiselessly, they waited for the artillery barrage to signal their rush forwards. Presently, the grey dawn tranquillity was shattered by the crash and shriek of impacting shells. Von Pacsynksi's men sprang forwards, running with the distinctive crouch of an infantryman in contact. British Vickers guns, eight of which came up during the night, added their laboured but persistent clatter to the din, striking the northern slopes of Bourlon Wood with heavy .303in. rounds.

This was the first of a series of concerted thrusts that morning. Every bit the equal of yesterday's struggle, it is small wonder that the Germans went on to call it *Das Ringen um Bourlon* – the wrestle at Bourlon. As before, Plunkett's obstinate followers flatly refused to relinquish their holes amongst the splintered trees.

Woollcombe cancelled 121st Brigade's attack at 0900hrs because he judged the available tank and infantry forces to be inadequate for the task of capturing Bourlon. A postponement of 24 hours was necessary. In a classically tragic failure of World War I communications, German artillery had cut the brigade's field telephone lines and the message never reached them. Consequently, they launched as planned. I Battalion's 12 tanks entered Bourlon about 200m ahead of the Highland Light Infantry and were driven out quickly with eight losses. German infantry were becoming much more confident in dealing with tanks. Barricades were used to force a halt while the tank's gearsmen engaged a turn, whereupon infantry would approach from the rear and stuff charges beneath its tracks. By contrast, the Highlanders' three lead companies infiltrated all the way to the railway line at the north-east end of Bourlon. Such dynamic progress was enabled by bypass of principal German strongpoints.

The Suffolks were less fortunate and stopped up against a fiendish network of machine-gun positions, pre-registered mortar killing areas and mobile squads of aggressive infantry. By 1700hrs, they had withdrawn to the start line. One company of Highland Light Infantry with battalion headquarters failed to join the others and became cut off in the south-east side of Bourlon. They were going to have to spend the night there.

At 1615hrs, Plunkett's desperate band finally threw the last of the German attacks off the northern end of Bourlon Wood. That night, 2nd/Scots Guards and two companies of 40th Division's 11th/King's Own Royal Lancaster Regiment were brought up to replace the day's losses.

BEGINNING OF THE END

Haig was losing patience. He could not fathom IV Corps' inability to achieve its objectives. Byng was given 2nd and 47th (2nd London) Divisions and told to take personal control. Up until now Woollcombe had largely been left to his own devices. Third Army's contribution was allocation and management of resources. It is not clear what more Byng

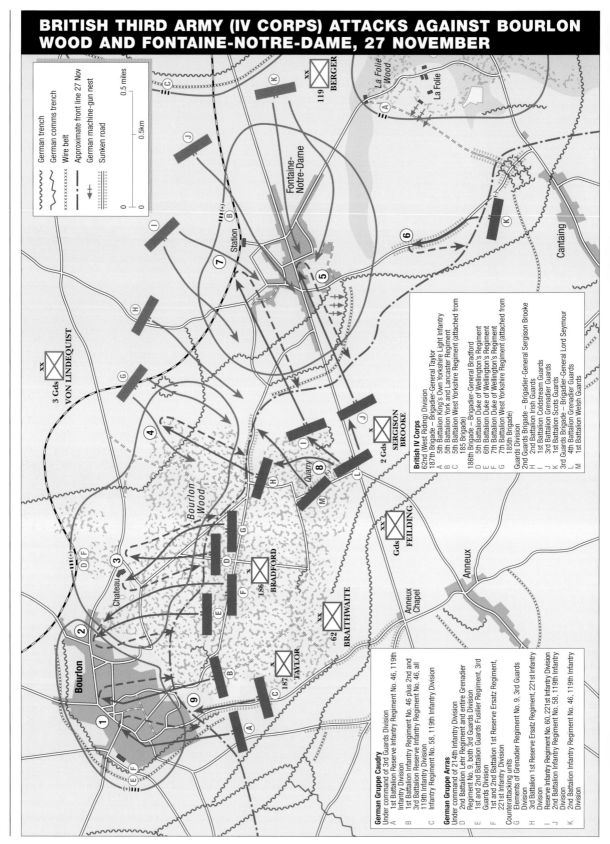

German trench

German comms trench

Wire belt

Approximate front line 27 Nov

German machine-gun nest

Sunken road

0.5 miles

0.5km

0 0.5km

German Gruppe Caudry
Under command of 3rd Guards Division
A 1st Battalion Reserve Infantry Regiment No. 46, 119th Infantry Division
B 1st Battalion Infantry Regiment No. 46 plus 2nd and 3rd Battalion Reserve Infantry Regiment No. 46, all 119th Infantry Division
C Infantry Regiment No. 58, 119th Infantry Division

German Gruppe Arras
Under command of 214th Infantry Division
D 2nd Battalion Lehr Regiment and entire Grenadier Regiment No. 9, both 3rd Guards Division
E 1st and 2nd Battalion Guards Fusilier Regiment, 3rd Guards Division
F 1st and 2nd Battalion 1st Reserve Ersatz Regiment, 221st Infantry Division
Counterattacking units
G Elements of Grenadier Regiment No. 9, 3rd Guards Division
H 3rd Battalion 1st Reserve Ersatz Regiment, 221st Infantry Division
I Reserve Infantry Regiment No. 60, 221st Infantry Division
J 2nd Battalion Infantry Regiment No. 58, 119th Infantry Division
K 2nd Battalion Infantry Regiment No. 46, 119th Infantry Division

British IV Corps
62nd (West Riding) Division
187th Brigade – Brigadier-General Taylor
A 5th Battalion King's Own Yorkshire Light Infantry
B 5th Battalion York and Lancaster Regiment
C 5th Battalion West Yorkshire Regiment (attached from 185th Brigade)
186th Brigade – Brigadier-General Bradford
D 5th Battalion Duke of Wellington's Regiment
E 6th Battalion Duke of Wellington's Regiment
F 7th Battalion Duke of Wellington's Regiment
G 7th Battalion West Yorkshire Regiment (attached from 185th Brigade)
Guards Division
2nd Guards Brigade – Brigadier-General Sergison Brooke
H 2nd Battalion Irish Guards
I 1st Battalion Coldstream Guards
J 3rd Battalion Grenadier Guards
K 1st Battalion Scots Guards
3rd Guards Brigade – Brigadier-General Lord Seymour
L 4th Battalion Grenadier Guards
M 1st Battalion Welsh Guards

and his staff could contribute, save lobbying higher command for even more manpower. More conspicuous in its absence during this operation was the intelligence effort.[15] With Rupprecht pumping reserves into the Cambrai sector as preparation for operational (as opposed to local) counterattack, it suited him that the British should be hurling themselves at Bourlon Ridge in such costly fashion. With all Elles' tanks now withdrawn for refit, cavalry being pressed into the infantry role and the drained 62nd Division sent *back into the line* to replace a virtually obliterated 40th Division, it must have been evident that Operation *GY* was on its last legs. All one can say in their defence is that withdrawal (which was the only other realistic option) would have meant it had all been in vain. The beguiling question being: surely one last push could carry the day? This attitude is understandable. Plunkett and the trapped Highlanders in Bourlon would certainly have agreed.

It was settled. Third Army started cultivating plans for an attack on 27 November. In the meantime, 40th Division's last uncommitted battalion, 13th East Surreys, were going to attempt a relief of the Highland Light Infantry first thing in the morning; an unenviable mission. Fear of fratricide precluded bombardment and there were no tanks. Relying on speed and stealth, their dawn dash succeeded in reaching the Highlanders' battalion headquarters but it stirred up a hard-hitting counterattack. There was no way that the force by the railway would be reached and it was just as well that nobody died trying – ammunition expended, they had surrendered at 0930hrs. The Surreys' commanding officer, Lieutenant-Colonel Warden, combined effort with the remaining Highlanders (whose own Colonel had been killed that morning), organized a defence and fought skilfully through the day.

The indefatigable Plunkett spent another day in action, repelling repeated attempts by 3rd Guards Division to rout him. Such laconic reportage conceals so much; the incredible reserves of stamina and courage required to sustain this baneful existence in a fringe of woodland. Generalleutnant von Lindequist commanding 3rd Guards sent a frustrated signal to von Moser reading: 'In spite of all endeavours, the British cannot be driven out of the wood'. For the men 62nd Division relieved that night, 23 November must have seemed a lifetime ago. Warden remained in Bourlon – extrication being too perilous.

---

15 Third Army reported the arrival of 119th, 214th and 3rd Guards Divisions three days after they first went into action at Cambrai.

Fontaine as viewed from the start line of the 3rd/Grenadier Guards. Machine-gun fire from La Folie Wood was so fierce that only seven men out of the two lead companies reached the church visible on the right. (Author's collection)

Attacking through Bourlon Wood, the Irish Guards reported it 'alive with concealed machine guns' that had to be cleared by bomb and bayonet. This is one of them. (Regimental Collection, Irish Guards)

26 November was set aside for a euphemistic 'recuperation', giving the heavy artillery an opportunity to pulverize even more of the once sleepy villages like Bourlon, Moeuvres and Fontaine. Hunkered down in their malodorous dugouts, the stoic German infantry were suffering. One candid junior officer's letter from Bourlon illuminates:

> *With the current weather conditions my platoon will soon have to fight off a new enemy. Every night we are moved about in the snow and rain and then spend the whole day squatting in our holes, nearly turning to ice in wet clothes. If we are to stay any longer in this place, I pray that we are sent some more schnapps at least.*[16]

Such parochial concerns were beyond the agenda of a high-level conference taking place that morning at Graincourt. Haig, Byng and Woollcombe arrived to discuss tomorrow's attack with Major-Generals Braithwaite (commanding 62nd Division) and Feilding (commanding the Guards Division). The plan was straightforward: 62nd would have another crack at Bourlon with 20 refurbished tanks and the Guards would take Fontaine with the assistance of another 12.

There was a tense atmosphere. Feilding judged his task to be impossible and was saying so. He had seen what had happened to the 51st with 36 tanks. Moreover, Fontaine had since been reinforced. Surely, he implored, it would be better to withdraw to Flesquières Ridge for the winter. His forceful case was deflected with platitudes and he returned to his division forlorn. A light snow fell, muffling the incessant thud and crump of preparatory shelling.

'A DIRTY AND A NOISY PLACE WAS BOURLON'

Despite a full day to prepare, most of the attacking companies did not receive their orders until midnight. There was no chance to survey the ground or rehearse with tanks. Consequently, Feilding's plan was necessarily orthodox – 2nd Guards Brigade was going take on Fontaine with their left extreme (2nd/Irish Guards) actually inside Bourlon Wood hoping to retake the north-east corner lost on 24 November. On the right, he tasked 2nd/Scots Guards to sweep down from Cantaing. 3rd Guards Brigade was in reserve.

Events transpired much as Feilding predicted. Advancing at 0620hrs under a creeping barrage, 1st/Coldstream Guards and 3rd/ Grenadier Guards managed to get into Fontaine with the tanks from F and I Battalion but street fighting is cruelly expensive; casualties soon mounted. German defenders from 46th Regiment 'hunted the tanks with enthusiasm'[17] but they too suffered. F41, 'Fray Bentos' accounted for 40 men before succumbing. Now also wise to German tactics, the remainder survived. In the wood, the Irish Guards lost cohesion and direction but arrived at their objective through pure obstinacy. Emerging from the sunken road that leads out of Cantaing, the Scots Guards were decimated by machine guns, just as their countrymen had been the week before. Sergeant John McAulay, who carried his wounded commander 400m, delivered the lead company to safety. Where objectives were achieved (in north Fontaine and in Bourlon Wood), crushing counterattacks drove the Guards back. Reserves were pushed into the line in response but Feilding saw no value in reinforcing failure. It was over by 1000hrs. They withdrew and bedraggled survivors limped back throughout the day.

The 62nd Division had a similarly unequal battle, attacking Bourlon from the wood with 186th Brigade and from the south with 187th. On both fronts, fighting was fierce. Nineteen tanks crossed the start line in support, 11 on the left and eight on the right. Unlike Fontaine very few got out, just five. German infantry drew them into murderous ambushes utilizing stubby-barrelled 7.6cm assault guns and ball charges. Bourlon was obscured by incessant German artillery bombardment, including use of gas shells in the British rear. The Duke of Wellington's battalions from 186th Brigade penetrated on a similar axis to the Highland Light Infantry, silencing a howitzer battery with the assistance of three C Battalion tanks. Better yet, Warden's East Surreys were reached and could withdraw at last. The only evidence of

Major-General Sir Geoffrey Feilding (centre) with King George V and Field Marshal Haig. Adamant that his Guards Division's attack against Fontaine was futile, he recommended withdrawal to the Flesquières Ridge – a view that ultimately was vindicated. (IWM Q 944)

---

17 German dispatch quoted in *Bourlon Wood*, Jack Horstall and Nigel Cave.

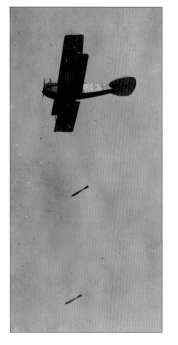

the Highlanders was their corpses. 5th/King's Own Yorkshire Light Infantry and 5th/Yorkshire and Lancashire Regiment of 187th Brigade became separated, allowing the Germans to flank them from a wedge in between. The pointlessness of this attack was manifestly clear by mid-morning and Braithwaite ordered a withdrawal to prepare for the habitual German counterattack, which was repulsed by 186th Brigade that afternoon.

On hearing the news, Haig called a stop. The 2nd, 47th (London) and 59th (2nd North Midland) Divisions were ordered forward, not to attack but to relieve the 36th, 62nd and Guards respectively. These shattered formations would remain in the vicinity as reserves while Byng reorganized the front for winter. Precarious as it was, they opted to hang onto the occupied areas of Bourlon for the time being as it was imperative to screen preparations for a long-term defensive line on Flesquières Ridge (Feilding must have shook his head on discovering that). Byng gave Woollcombe the freedom to mount local attacks up the Canal du Nord if this could create a defensive advantage. He did not exercise it.

RUPPRECHT'S TURN

These decisions were unbeknown to Rupprecht. That very day, he was in conference with the German High Commander, General Ludendorff, to discuss their long-awaited counterstroke. Forming two new *Gruppen* – Lewarde north of Gruppe Arras and Busigny south of Gruppe Caudry – Northern Army Group could concentrate an extra seven divisions on the Cambrai front to augment those already committed to action. Echoing British thinking earlier in the year, they opted for a northerly thrust to cut the salient created by Byng's advance. The main effort was recapture of the Siegfried Stellung front lines. Rupprecht issued his operation order to von der Marwitz that night:

1. Attack on 30 November.
2 . Main blow by eastern Gruppen, general direction Metz [west], capturing Flesquières and Havrincourt Wood from the south in order to take British in flank and rear.
3. Attack of Gruppe Arras to be delivered [after main stroke of eastern Gruppen] from west of Bourlon towards the south. Recommended that Gruppe Arras begin artillery fire and demonstrations as early as possible in order to pin down enemy forces on its front. Etc …

Rupprecht's greatest fear was a British advance in Masnières – he had to operate under the assumption that cessation of Byng's effort was temporary. The plan was developed with his *Gruppe* commanders over the next 24 hours.

Gruppe Busigny, under Generalleutnant von Kathen, would attack with three fresh divisions – 183rd, 208th and 34th – between Banteux and Vendhuille. The 183rd was in the line on 20 November but largely bypassed to the north. Von Watter's Gruppe Caudry was to their north, with 28th, 220th, 30th and 107th Divisions. Only the latter had yet been in action at Cambrai. These were the 'eastern' *Gruppen* described in the above operations order. Having penetrated as far as Havrincourt and its wood, they planned to swing north, rolling up Third Army's front and meeting von Moser's Gruppe Arras on its way south with 119th, 214th, 221st and 49th Reserve Divisions. With the exception of 221st and 49th Reserve, this *Gruppe* had previously been committed to battle. The absence of 3rd Guards betrays their exhaustion.

Rupprecht was right to have been patient. Although Byng also had three rested divisions now in the line (four if you count 55th Division in VII Corps area at the southern end of Rupprecht's breach), the Germans had overwhelming superiority on their primary axis over a depleted III Corps. Crucially, Second Army now enjoyed the firepower of 1,200 artillery pieces.

28 November brought milder weather and with it mist, concealing much of German preparation from the prying eyes of the Royal Flying Corps. Nevertheless, such a massive build-up, being less calculated than Byng's in the run-up to *GY*, did not escape notice. VII Corps were especially jumpy. Lieutenant-General Sir Thomas D'Oyly Snow had signalled his concerns to Byng as long ago as 25 November. These

observations were not ignored but, when von Moser opened a gas and high-explosive barrage of Bourlon Wood on 28 November, it merely encouraged the perception that this was the threatened sector. Third Army were also reading GHQ intelligence summaries assessing German strength as too low to permit large-scale attack. Indisputably, complacency prevailed. No Army-level warning order was issued to reserves or front-line positions.

Anyhow, 55th Division in the line at Banteux made preparations to resist any offensive. Its commander, Major-General Jeudwine ordered the creation of a backstop strongpoint in Villers Guislan and prepared pre-emptive artillery missions for the morning of 30 November. At much the same time on the evening of 29 November as Byng was holding a dinner to celebrate his promotion to substantive General, the 5th/South Lancashire Regiment of 166th Brigade holding Banteux Ravine received a signal: 'In the event of attack you will hold the line at all costs. There is to be no retirement to any second line. Warn all ranks to be specially alert.'[18]

ANGRIFFSCHLACHT

When the blow fell, chaos spread like a contagion. Gruppe Busigny opened a barrage at 0600hrs that was deceivingly sporadic – probably designed to confuse the British whether or not they were under attack. Building rapidly in intensity, the first groups of assaulting infantry came on in rushes shortly after 0700hrs. The Germans spearheaded their offensive with *Sturmbataillone* – Gruppe Busigny using the 3rd Jäger Battalion. Retreating infantry reported a proliferation of light machine guns and some flame-throwers. Banteux Ravine was overrun in short order, its Vickers emplacements pummelled by a flurry of mortar shells that *Stosstruppen* scuttled under as if invulnerable. Aircraft buzzed and swooped like hungry gulls. The German onslaught bypassed pockets of resistance; a policy that bred the term 'infiltration' tactics. Mist added to the confusion in scenes richly reminiscent of 20 November: distress flares arcing haphazardly into the dawn, forward positions failing to answer field telephones, erroneous and contradictory reports.

The 183rd Division drove hard down the boundary between 55th and 12th Divisions and these two formations bore the brunt. The right of Jeudwine's command (164th Brigade) was spared all but the barrage. His centre brigade, 165th, marked the southern end of Rupprecht's offensive and its northernmost battalion, 6th/King's Regiment, fought all day to anchor the line. 166th Brigade, whose front included Banteux Ravine, was washed away. Of its three battalions in the line, only 10th/King's repulsed the attacks long enough to make a second stand in the support line. 5th/North Lancashire and 5th/South Lancashire were enveloped; in the latter 'barely a man survived'.[19]

Jeudwine kept his cool, reinforcing the anchor with reserve battalions and creating improvised fighting units from road building parties. He

---

18 British official history, *The Battle of Cambrai 1917*, Captain Wilfred Miles.
19 Ibid.

even mounted a counterattack against German second echelon columns.

The 12th Division was disadvantaged straight away because the deluge of German infantry on the Banteux axis flowed into its flanks, cutting off forward positions. The 35th Brigade was manning a frontage of 3km and its commander, Brigadier-General Vincent, had no contact with his forward battalions from the start. Shelling had cut his telephone lines. Brigade headquarters was in the village of Villers-Guislan and leading German infantry units from 34th Division arrived there as early as 0730hrs. Hence Vincent found himself fighting before he even knew what had befallen his command. Shepherding a motley group of clerks, staff officers and sappers, he conducted a fighting withdrawal towards Gauche Wood. Soon evicted from that refuge by artillery, 'Vincent's Force' (as it came to be known) worked its way to some high ground farther west, collecting more stragglers in the process.

Meanwhile, his battalions were being wiped out. The reserve battalion, 7th/Suffolks, was being attacked east of Gonnelieu at the same time as his forward elements, 5th/Royal Berkshires and 7th/Norfolks. Theirs is a familiar tale of desperate resistance. War diaries speak of the battalions doing 'great execution' with their small arms but 35th Brigade was undermanned and spread far too thin to stem the tide of an entire division. All three commanding officers were among the dead and missing.

The slopes around Gonnelieu and Villers-Guislan were also home to a large number of artillery batteries. Displaying a stubbornness that cost many a gunner his life that morning, field and heavy batteries alike engaged the oncoming infantry over open sights, reaping a terrible harvest. Removing breeches and sights at the last safe moment, they then fought as infantry.

None of this prevented Gruppe Busigny from capturing Gouzeaucourt, 5km behind British lines, at about 1000hrs. Unfortunately, the doggedness of so many individuals – long after the collapse of formal command and control structures – was not part of Rupprecht and von der Marwitz' narrative. Perhaps they should have recalled the exploits of Major Krebbs *et al*. British and German troops are not so different. It had been a long morning for everybody. Already his men were tiring and they paused in the centre of Gouzeaucourt to gorge themselves on a captured supply convoy.

For all his earlier complacency, Byng displayed laudable sangfroid and reacted decisively. Tank battalions being entrained at Flins were ordered to get as many into action as possible. The Guards Division was placed under command of III Corps but its 1st Brigade made straight for Gouzeaucourt. Sensing that the German thrust was directed at Metz, Kavanagh's Cavalry Corps was ordered to support VII Corps by counterattacking from the south-west in order to cut off its head.

Both attacks were delivered in stereotypical fashion. The 5th Cavalry Division made a bid for Villers-Guislan. The 8th Hussars from Ambala Brigade joined the 12th Hussars of 5th Brigade in a dashing gallop for Gauche Wood. Driven back by machine-gun fire, they dismounted along with Hodson's Horse and pressed home another audacious attack, this time consolidating on Chapel Hill. For their part, the 1st Guards Brigade arrived west of Gouzeaucourt at 1230hrs. Passing retreating stragglers, 'the advance over the downland of the three battalions in

LEFT *Stosstruppen* training with a medium 17cm Minenwerfer. Man-hauled into battle by a crew of four, these weapons provided indirect fire support to the assault squads. Live training enabled them to bring the rounds in incredibly close to friendly troops (IWM Q 23754)

perfect order was a heartening sight'.[20] Recapture of the town was equally efficient and, within half an hour, they were preparing defences on its eastern flank.

Gruppe Caudry's drive for Metz enjoyed all the same advantages of surprise and concentration of force but the ground was not as kind. No sooner had they crossed the St Quentin Canal north of Banteux, they ran into 36th and 37th Brigades of 12th Division rooted to the very same network of fortified farm buildings that had delayed III Corps on 20 November: Bleak House, Le Pavé, Pam Pam, Le Quennet and Bonavis. Here too, the defenders sold themselves dear, counterattacking as soon as any opportunity arose. However, 28th and 220th Division were at full strength and rested, whereas the defending battalions were heavily depleted. This was their undoing. Eventually, the strongly defended farms were bypassed, leaving defenders to cause as much trouble as possible until ammunition was expended. Survivors fell back on the thick (German-built) defences around La Vacquerie, which became a rallying point for all manner of British forces. Stretching the range of supporting artillery, even determined, assault-trained infantry could not get into it. German accounts express disappointment at this, blaming the seemingly superhuman steadfastness of its defenders.

28th Division's left flank had fared better, essentially forming part of Gruppe Busigny's capture of Gonnelieu. Their inclination to press north of the town and onto Villers-Plouich may well have flanked La Vacquerie had it not been for the arrival of the Light Infantry of 60th Brigade – 20th Division's reserve – who became embroiled as the mêlée drifted into its flank. Their comrades farther forwards clashed with Gruppe Caudry's 220th Division, making for Couillet Wood. 59th and 61st Brigades were prejudiced by forward slope positions, enabling German aircraft and artillery to batter them with ease. Study of the detail would be repetitive. Suffice it to say that 10th/King's Royal Rifle Corps (59th Brigade) limped into La Vacquerie that night with 20 men.

On the north side of his frontage, von Watter was issued a cruel reminder of how easy it had been to block Byng at Masnières and Marcoing. Fittingly, it came from the very same division that he had thwarted – 29th. At 0900hrs, 107th Division emerged from Siegfried II

OPPOSITE
1. The Germans intend to cut off the British-held salient at its southern end and then roll it up northwards towards Flesquières. The main effort is in the area of Banteux to Villers-Guislan, with a second focal point in the ground west of Bourlon Wood.
2. The German attacks on the Banteux/Villers-Guislan front meet initial success, forcing a British retirement of two to three miles. The British rally on a line roughly parallel with the railway east of Gouzeaucourt.
3. The attacks north of Bonavis overrun British forward positions but fail to provoke a full retreat.
4. The attackers astride the boundary between Gruppen Arras and Caudry make no headway. The British machine-gunners decimate assaulting infantry in the low ground south-west of Fontaine-Notre-Dame.
5. The fighting near the Canal du Nord is equally bitter. Unable to breakthrough, von Moser keeps pressing until the 7 December British withdrawal to a consolidated line.
6. Von Kathen's Gruppe Busigny resumes the offensive down in Gouzeaucourt on 1 December. The effort is blunted by counterattacks from the Guards and two divisions of the Cavalry Corps. Gauche Wood is recaptured but the Germans hold onto Villers-Guislan.
7. Fighting also continues around Marcoing and Masnières that day and again on 3 December. Eventually, it is decided that the British 29th Division positions north of the St Quentin canal are untenable. They are withdrawn as part of the general retirement conducted between 4 and 7 December.

20 British Official History, *The Battle of Cambrai 1917*, Captain Wilfrid Miles.

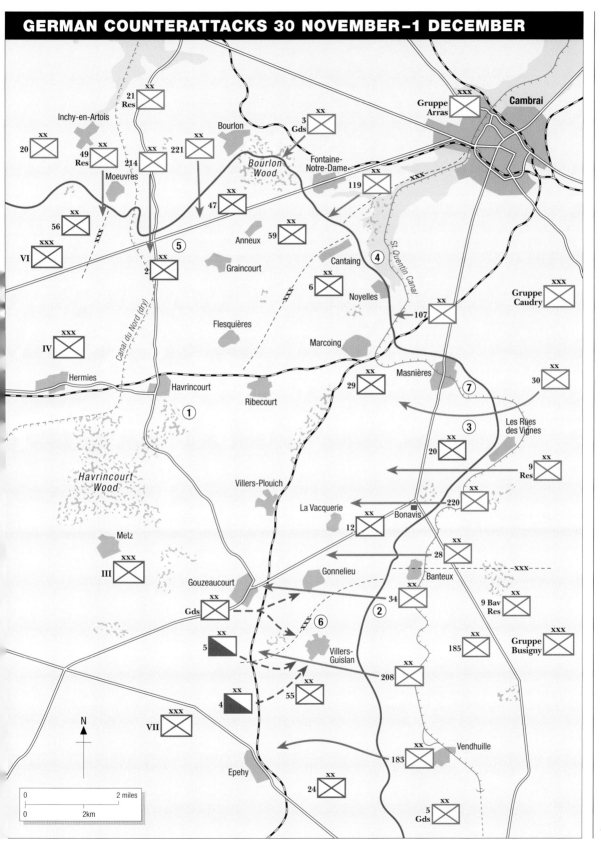

21 Res

Inchy-en-Artois

Bourlon

3 Gds

Gruppe Arras

Cambrai

20

49 Res

214

221

Fontaine-Notre-Dame

Moeuvres

Bourlon Wood

119

56

VI

47

Anneux

59

2

5

Graincourt

Cantaing

4

St Quentin Canal

Gruppe Caudry

IV

Canal du Nord (dry)

Flesquières

6

Noyelles

107

Marcoing

Hermies

Havrincourt

Ribecourt

Masnières

29

7

30

1

Les Rues des Vignes

3

20

9 Res

Havrincourt Wood

Villers-Plouich

La Vacquerie

Bonavis

220

Metz

12

28

III

Gouzeaucourt

Gonnelieu

Banteux

9 Bav Res

Gds

34

2

185

Gruppe Busigny

5

6

Villers-Guislan

208

4

55

VII

N

183

Vendhuille

Epehy

24

5 Gds

| 0 | | 2 miles |
| 0 | | 2km |

into a murderous fire. None of their regiments made it to within 400m of 86th Brigade's line. The gravest threat developed from another quarter. 61st Brigade's collapse south of Les Rues Vertes presented 30th Division with an opportunity to trap the British on the north side of the canal. Major-General de Lisle was powerless to influence events; 29th Division's headquarters had been overrun by Gruppe Busigny's uppercut at 0845hrs and he was on the run. Predictably for 30 November, their salvation fell to a miniscule party of defenders led by Captain Gee, an 86th Brigade staff officer. He won a Victoria Cross for a catalogue of adventures, driving the lead assault force out of the village and silencing a machine gun they left there to pin him down. By the time the 99th Regiment (30th Division lead) could respond in force, Gee had created a stalwart redoubt. The 88th Brigade in divisional reserve established even stronger defensive positions south of Marcoing Copse, which it used as the springboard for a series of counterattacks through the day.

Cantaing and Fontaine were excused the worst of the fighting as they lay between the two principal German axes. Two diversionary attacks were made by 119th Division's 46th and 58th Regiments (who had been fighting since 21 November) at 0900hrs and 1100hrs. Both were stopped in their tracks by 176th Brigade of 59th Division holding that line. Akin to Masnières, there was a cruel justice in the erstwhile defenders of Fontaine emerging to die in the same manner as their Scottish victims.

In Bourlon Wood, 30 November dawned with a gas barrage. Thudding into the ground like duds, the shells vented phosgene, a heavier-than-air choking agent that smells of fresh-cut hay. Inhabiting the wood was the right-hand brigade of 47th Division, the 141st. Drifting downhill, the phosgene settled so densely in the area of 19th/London Regiment that only 70 men remained fit for duty. At midday, forward positions were attacked by the extraordinarily resilient 3rd Guards Division regiments. In a work of fiction they might finally have vanquished the wood but this is reality. They were hurled back.

Instead, von Moser's Gruppe Arras delivered its 'hammer blow' farther west, massing three divisions – 214th, 221st and 49th Reserve – to sweep down onto Graincourt on a 4km frontage. Standing in their way were three brigades of British infantry: 140th Brigade from 47th Division, occupying the left side of Bourlon Wood below the village; 99th Brigade from 2nd Division, east of the Canal du Nord in the old Siegfried Stellung support line; 6th Brigade, left flank of 2nd Division west of the canal below Moeuvres. Approximately 12,000 infantrymen against a British force of about 3,000.

They came on in similar fashion to the eastern *Gruppen*: rushes of *Stosstruppen* preceding a congestion of infantry. However, unlike Banteux, there were no covered approaches and Byng had predicted attack on this front. The heavy batteries put in place to support his Bourlon Wood operation were still in position. The massive available firepower exacted a grave price. In scenes comparable to Verdun, shrapnel and high explosive tore into the packed ranks with a brutal indifference. Enfilading machine guns worked from both flanks, one eight-gun Vickers detachment firing 70,000 rounds. The 92nd Regiment were labouring towards the Anneux Sugar Factory:

Gruppe Arras attacked astride the dry Canal du Nord. A pair of imposing lock gates are in the distance. Spare a thought for the amount of backbreaking spadework required to build that sandbag bridge in the foreground. (Regimental Collection, Irish Guards)

Gruppe Arras attacked astride the dry Canal du Nord. A pair of imposing lock gates are in the distance. Spare a thought for the amount of backbreaking spadework required to build that sandbag bridge in the foreground. (Regimental Collection, Irish Guards)

Vickers machine gun sections [in Bourlon Wood] formed an immense wall of fire. The enemy was not disposed to leave this powerful strongpoint. Beside machine guns, there were sharpshooters whose single shots [fired] at the line of the regiment as soon as a head was visible.[21]

Grit and sheer volume of manpower carried the Germans forwards. A gap was found between the 99th and 140th Brigades, which *Stosstruppen* ferreted into, flanking 6th/London Regiment. That battalion was overwhelmed and their neighbours, the 5th Battalion, were compelled to withdraw to an oblique position along the west side of Bourlon Wood. Immediate counterattack by 8th and 15th/London Regiment restored order in the nick of time. Forward positions across 2nd Division's line were destroyed or cut off and main defensive positions endured similar pressure. The 1st/Royal Berkshire and 17th/Royal Fusiliers east of the canal were pushed back until shored up by the timely arrival of 99th Brigade's reserve 23rd/Royal Fusiliers. West of the Canal, 6th Brigade had 13th/Essex Regiment forwards. Here the gulley formed by the dry lock bed shielded the attacking 226th Reserve Regiment from the worst of enfilade fire and they wrestled for an improvised strongpoint constructed around lock gates (Lock Number 5). The 13th/Essex lost the gates but the Germans could progress no farther. West of the canal, 1st/King's Regiment clung all day to their patch, assisted by a mix of reserve units and 56th Division's machine guns.

Engulfed by the German advance, the survivors of one company from 13th/Essex made a unanimous decision to fight to the death rather than surrender. This staggering level of commitment is perhaps difficult to empathize with today but it reflects the fatalism engendered by exposure to the horrors of trench warfare. Life was cheap.

As night fell on 30 November, Rupprecht's offensive was already losing momentum. Consoling himself with the observation that 'if the success is not so great as we hoped, it has nevertheless given the British a blow'[22], he prepared a renewed effort on the morrow. Gruppe Arras was mired in the Moeuvres–Bourlon gap and one of its divisions, 221st,

21 *Angriffschlacht bei Cambrai*, 92nd Infantry Regiment Official History.
22 British Official History, *The Battle of Cambrai 1917*, Captain Wilfrid Miles.

ANGRIFFSCHLACHT – *STOSSTRUPPEN* ON CANAL DU NORD, 1 DECEMBER 1917 (pages 82–83)

German assault troops from 73rd Hanoverian Infantry Regiment's *Sturmbataillone* (operating as part of 49th Reserve Infantry Division) attacking 13th Battalion Essex Regiment (6th Brigade, 2nd Division) at 0730hrs, 1 December 1917. This sector of the battlefield ran astride the Canal du Nord. Instead of fighting from perpendicular opposing trenches, the combatants duelled and scrapped up the old Siegfried Stellung support line parallel to Gruppe Arras' axis. This created an environment well suited to the aggressive and dynamic 'infiltration' tactics being applied by the spearheading *Stosstruppen*.

The basic grouping within assault companies was the 18-man section, divided into two squads of nine – the assault *Gruppe*. The primary weapon for close-quarter combat was the grenade, carried in Hessian sacks under the arms (1). Sections were also scaled for a Maxim 08/15 light machine gun, which provided intimate suppressive fire (2). Orchestration was the essence of it. Such small units were able to make headway because their attacks were coordinated with judicious application of firepower. Inherent limitations in communication were overcome by making support assets organic. *Sturmbataillone* were equipped with flamethrowers, mortars, stubby direct-fire assault guns and twice the usual allocation of Maxim medium machine guns. Field artillery perfected the 'lightning barrage', firing less accurate unregistered shells but with the aim of simply suppressing rather than destroying enemy positions. The *Stosstruppen* are carrying just enough equipment to sustain them without undue encumbrance. Shovels are universal; reflecting the imperative for consolidation once the advance had culminated.

Here the first squad is working its way down the barricaded (3) trench system. A flurry of grenades will cover the rush by men armed with bayonets and sharpened entrenching tools (4). Meanwhile, the second squad is attempting to bypass the point of resistance protected by the battalion's integral mortars (5). The British Lewis gun that poses the greatest threat to that manoeuvre is being neutralized by first squad's Maxim 08/15 (6). Such dynamic synchronization was achieved by perilous training that majored on teaching troops to anticipate; hence extra ammunition is being offered to the gun group before they have called for it (7). Nevertheless, the narrow battlefield levelled the odds. In his memoir, *Storm of Steel*, 73rd Hanoverian Regiment *Sturmkompanie* commander Ernst Jünger describes his experience of this attack: 'The British resisted manfully. Every traverse had to be fought for. The black balls of Mills bombs crossed in the air with our own long-handled grenades. Behind every traverse we captured we found corpses or bodies still twitching ... We too suffered losses. A piece of iron crashed to the ground, which a fellow was unable to avoid; and he collapsed to the ground, while his blood issued on to the clay from his many wounds.' (Illustration by Peter Dennis)

was already a spent force. There was nothing more to do up there except push on metre by metre. Eastern *Gruppen* had 9th Bavarian Reserve and 185th Divisions to commit. They would continue on the primary axis beyond Gouzeaucourt, supported by subsidiary attacks on Couillet Wood (9th Reserve), Gauche Wood (208th and 183rd) and La Vacquerie (34th). Pressure would be maintained on Masnières–Les Rue Vertes but Fontaine and Cantaing were out of it. 119th and 3rd Guards Divisions were now totally incapable of offensive operations.

Byng was not planning on waiting for the strike. He backstopped Moeuvres–Bourlon with 62nd Division (back in action yet again) and ordered dawn counterattacks: the Guards towards Gonnelieu and Cavalry against Gauche Wood. Thirty-nine tanks from H, B and A Battalions mustered in support. GHQ reacted by warning off Flanders-based divisions for relocation to the threatened Cambrai sector. The 5th Division's redeployment to Italy was frozen in order to free up rail capacity.

Byng's Z-Hour pre-empted Rupprecht's by two hours. Hence, when the Guards Division moved with 20 H Battalion tanks towards Gonnelieu, they encountered German infantry forming up – Bavarian infantry regiments with 4th Sturmbataillone attached – in what was effectively a meeting engagement. The 3rd Guards Brigade (4th/Grenadier Guards and 1st/Welsh Guards) were driven out of Gonnelieu but had succeeded in spoiling the German attack. Here the Guards fell back to the western outskirts. However, farther south the 3rd/Coldstream and 2nd/Grenadiers of 1st Guards Brigade had carried the ridge running from Gonnelieu down to Gauche Wood using their tanks to great effect. Here the operation tied in neatly with 5th Cavalry Division's dismounted attack on Gauche Wood by the 18th Lancers and Indians of Ambala Brigade. Three tanks even made it back into Villers-Guislan for a short time. Unfortunately for the Cavalry, it was inconclusive on their right flank, where a mixture of tanks, dismounted and mounted cavalry manoeuvred around unsuccessfully in a bid to retake Villers-Guislan from the south. Lacking artillery, they could not suppress accurate German machine-gun fire. 2nd Lancers charged with valour (jumping wire like huntsmen would a hedge) but to no avail. They lost momentum and were pinned down, exposed.

Most cavalry fighting to recapture Villers-Guislan did so dismounted but the 2nd Lancers charged in a bid to flank Villers Ridge from the south. They routed some Germans in Napoleonic fashion before the reminiscence was interrupted by machine-gun fire, halting the advance. (Regimental Collection, Irish Guards)

It kept attacking regiments occupied though and only at La Vacquerie were the Germans able to mount their operation unmolested. Battle raged all day, involving the remnants of 60th Brigade and 1st/Grenadier Guards. The battered hamlet assumed a symbolic quality, attracting the effort of German units that ought to have bypassed. It was a vicious affair. Fortunes shifted but by nightfall, the British held the Siegfried Stellung front-line positions 500m to the east.

Les Rues Vertes and Masnières took another hammering. Gruppe Caudry's 30th Division focused on seeking to isolate 29th Division north of the St Quentin Canal once more. Thus 86th Brigade (holding the bend in the canal) bore the brunt of it. They

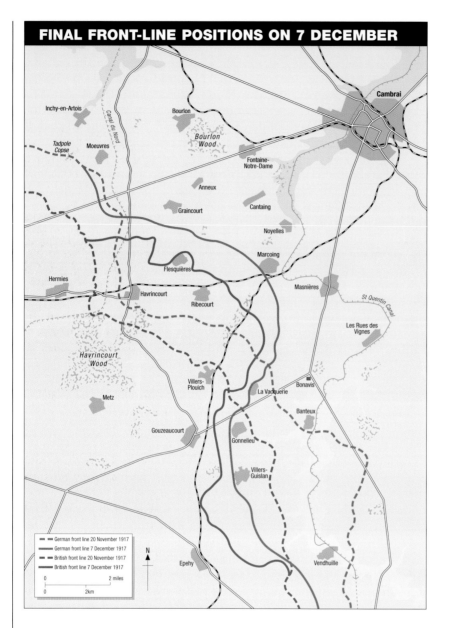

Legend:
- German front line 20 November 1917
- German front line 7 December 1917
- British front line 20 November 1917
- British front line 7 December 1917

0   2 miles
0   2km

resisted but at such cost that Brigadier-General Lucas opted to withdraw from the rubble of Masnières that night.

Day two had assumed the character of two exhausted boxers in a sweaty embrace. Neither protagonist possessed the wherewithal to craft anything decisive anymore; up on the Canal du Nord, they had spent the last 48 hours hurling hand grenades at each other with no demonstrable gain. Admitting that night that the offensive had 'run itself out', von der Marwitz pressed Rupprecht to shelve extravagant notions of envelopment and devote his attentions to fashioning an advantageous line for the winter.

Technically, 2 December was set aside for rest but this was ignored by von Watter – who attacked Marcoing – and von Moser who gave 2nd Division another shove south of Moeuvres. Neither made headway. On reflection, Rupprecht conceded that his designs had 'miscarried' and

endorsed von der Marwitz' emphasis. Haig and Byng reached an identical consensus. Early on 3 December, the two commanders appraised current dispositions and drafted the following telegram to the War Cabinet in London:

> *The present line could be held, but in view of the enemy's present activity it would use up troops, which, in view of your instructions and the manpower situation, I do not feel justified in devoting to it.*[23]

They would withdraw to the Flesquières line. A battle that had opened so suddenly a fortnight before now closed over the course of a week with a series of sporadic, localized contests for good ground.

Byng had been utilizing every available respite to improve Third Army's winter line and by 3 December it was in a fit state to be occupied. The withdrawal was executed with precision – the British have a peculiar talent for retreating in good order. At each stage rearguards were left behind to create an impression of activity so it would come as a surprise to the Germans opposite. But they too had a hand in the way it transpired.

Continued pressure encouraged III Corps to abandon La Vacquerie by 6 December; before dawn on 4 December, 29th Division were west of St Quentin Canal and joined the main withdrawal thereafter. The Bourlon and Cantaing front was pulled back gradually from 4 December, 47th Division bidding a wry farewell to Bourlon Wood by laying booby traps. Covering positions were used as an interim step and the line had been finalized by 7 December. The guns did not fall silent but 'such fighting as took place … during the remainder of the month may be regarded as incidental to active trench warfare.'[24]

---

23 British Official History, *The Battle of Cambrai 1917*, Captain Wilfrid Miles.
24 Ibid.

AFTERMATH

RECRIMINATION

The disappointment did not take long to find its voice. A War Cabinet in London that had celebrated such incredible gains on 20 November was anxious for Haig's account of how it had all unravelled so spectacularly ten days later. Tales of routed British troops discarding weapons demanded explanation. Reports were exacted from every command level, culminating in Parliamentary debate. Eventually, an independent inquiry was commissioned by the War Cabinet to be led by the eminent military authority General Smuts. It is beyond the scope of this study to chart the debate in detail but the principal conclusions warrant summary.

Rupprecht's counterattack had not been a surprise; all reasonable precautions had been taken. Of the three principal thrusts – Bourlon, Masnières and Gonnelieu – the third was the smallest. 'No one down to and including corps commanders was to blame … There had been surprising breakdown of the defence on the right of [Byng's] battle front.' The collapse was attributed to poor training of new drafts coupled with inexperience of junior officers and NCOs. In response, the Government informed Parliament that it was 'detrimental to the public interest to have a public discussion of the breakdown which undoubtedly occurred'.[25]

This misrepresentation of the facts can be traced directly back to Third Army's testimony. It was Byng and his staff that singled out junior ranks; a generalization which, given the evidence, appears profoundly iniquitous. Examination of his original report shows how he censured the Machine Gun Corps for lacking 'staunchness', claiming a dearth of *esprit de corps*. His biographer insists the observations have been taken out of context, explaining that Byng was criticizing training standards, not the men. In part the opinion can also be explained by various misrepresentations in the chain of reporting beneath him (accounts of retreating rabbles were exaggerated).

However, irrespective of emphasis, Byng's characteristic solidarity with his soldiers is absent. His testimony declined to accept personal responsibility for the training standards of Third Army and failed to stress the sacrifice of gallant souls who fought to the death. Furthermore, he was patently disingenuous about preparations for German counterattack and its eventual emphasis. Byng had ample latitude to account for the reverse without going on the attack. Weak GHQ intelligence reporting, overwhelming German numerical superiority at decisive points, a precedent of recent German offensive

---

25 The Enquiry Report, including this Hansard entry, is in the National Archives – WO 32/5095B.

focus on Bourlon and bad weather are all reasonable grounds for a defence. Instead it fell to Haig to display magnanimity.

> *Whatever view may be held on the foregoing ['staunchness' of infantry], I feel, after careful consideration that all blame for the mishap … must rest on my shoulders. It was I who decided on the 22nd that Bourlon Wood should be attacked … The occupation of this position at once increased our front and threw extra work on our troops. As events on the 30th show, many of the men were very tired and unable to resist the enemy's blow, as I believe they could have done had they been fresher.*[26]

Haig's humility aside, this analysis is nearer the mark. Of course, the 55th, 12th and 20th Divisions had not been engaged at Bourlon Wood but they had been in the line for a long time, they were undermanned and most of Third Army's resources were committed to the Bourlon sector. Most poignant of all is the German analysis, which abounds with references to Britain's robust and determined infantrymen frustrating progress of Rupprecht's offensive on all fronts.

ELUSIVE EXPLOITATION

In that vein, the Germans had their own disappointments to contend with. The great strides of 30 November – showcasing their latest offensive doctrine – were not sufficient to realize Rupprecht's operational intent. His subsidiary axes had been checked at enormous human cost and negligible territorial gain. The official *post mortem* criticized von der Marwitz for diffusing the attacking divisions across too wide an area. Ludendorff surmised that even the 'fresh' divisions were tired. On balance, they are being hard on themselves as 30 November was a counterattack, not a planned offensive. Thrown together in haste amid the fury of British efforts to capture Bourlon Ridge, it lacked the detailed planning that foresight would have afforded. Given these restraints, the scale and ferocity achieved was remarkable.

Conversely, Operation *GY* enjoyed meticulous preparation, genuine surprise and unprecedented initial success. Hence the subsequent failure to exploit has attracted the bulk of conjecture and historical analysis of Cambrai. Contemporary assessment was overshadowed by the Smuts Enquiry but post-operational reports make interesting reading. There are recurring references to overloaded or overextended communications networks and unfamiliarity with 'open warfare' once troops found themselves beyond the Siegfried Stellung. Lack of infantry reserves – one of the most popular explanations in modern books – does not feature directly. Instead, they cite overcrowding of artillery, cavalry and logistics units on the narrow front as responsible for impeding V Corps' access to the battlefield. It was held 32km away.

Intimidated by the formidableness of the Siegfried Stellung, Byng dedicated a greater proportion of forces (particularly tanks) to the initial assault than ultimately proved necessary, creating a steady attenuation of effort as the day wore on. Had too many tanks been held

---

26 National Archives – WO 158/52.

in reserve, they might not have created these openings in the first place but, in retrospect, one can see that excessive emphasis was placed on infantry consolidation. It is unfair to insist that commanders should have identified this at the time – consolidation was an essential discipline in trench warfare – but it is evident how much it diluted Byng's combat power at Cambrai.

The effect of all this was that follow-on forces ended up with unrealistic objectives. The 62nd Division is a case in point. Two brigades were responsible for the break-in and then consolidated in the support line beyond Havrincourt, leaving just one brigade (186th) to clear Graincourt and the vital approaches to Bourlon Ridge. The 6th and 12th Divisions were tasked with little more than building defensive flanks around III Corps.

Then there is topography. The St Quentin Canal proved to be a significant obstacle. Despite the fact that a 2km stretch of Siegfried II remained undefended through the afternoon of 20 November, III Corps could not get enough forces over the canal to penetrate it. Security measures had precluded extensive air reconnaissance and serviceable crossings were not identified. Consequently, the 29th Division could project only small and irregular groups. These were manageable even for the modest German scratch force holding the far bank. When Fuller had conceived his original raid, Cambrai was selected precisely because the St Quentin Canal would isolate the area and protect his south-eastern flank. The sword proved double edged.

Kavanagh's Cavalry Corps often draws criticism for not being vigorous or imaginative enough in moving forwards. Assembly areas were too far back. There is probably some truth in this but (mistakenly perhaps) they took their cue from the corps headquarters to which they were attached. Inherent limitations of battlefield communications rendered that process convoluted and tardy; messages from units in contact literally took hours to get back, often on foot. Contradictory content was assured because the reports had originated in the fog of battle for villages like Flesquières.

Arguably more relevant is cavalry's unsuitability for exploitation operations in the first place. Mounted action both on 20 November and 1 December was expensive in horses and men. For all their mobility, there was no protection. Proposed exploitation routes outranged supporting artillery and, had tanks been available, they would never have kept pace. Armoured car detachments and motorcycle machine-gun companies might have had more utility but they too were unable to hold ground physically.

Most World War I exploitation debates eventually bump up against the interior lines advantage enjoyed by defenders. *Eingreifentaktik* misfired at Cambrai but it did not fail. The British are a self-critical race and aversion to accepting the superiority of their enemies is a common trait. As demonstrated earlier in respect of Flesquières, von der Marwitz' divisions fought hard. Within 24 hours, reserves were flowing into the front at a rate Byng could not hope to compete with and the offensive spirit displayed by these units was just the precursor to Rupprecht's 30 November 'hammer blow'.

Thus it follows that Haig's decision to press with *GY* after 21 November was a costly act of folly. As his earlier confession of culpability infers, this placed Herculean demands on the troops' stamina. However, Haig's thinking was predicated on the perceived strategic necessity of offensive operations; with Russia defeated, Italy in disarray, the United States gearing up and the French still recovering from the summer 'mutiny', the onus rested on him. By throwing a handful of divisions at Bourlon Ridge, he preoccupied the entire Northern Army Group. Doubtless, this was small comfort for the men dying in there but such is the cold arithmetic of grand strategy.

THE BIRTH OF ARMOURED WARFARE

Operation *GY* was probably destined to be strategically inconclusive. A more constructive application of hindsight is to examine its tremendous significance to the conceptual development of armoured warfare. Unsurprisingly, it will always best be remembered as the first application of massed armour; the tank's debut as an *operational* asset. This is true. Nevertheless, as has been demonstrated, in 1917 the Mark IV tank was still defined as much by its limitations as its capabilities. Obstacle crossing, wire crushing and direct fire support to infantry were there in abundance but so too were ponderous manoeuvrability, poor protection and firepower hamstrung by limited target acquisition. Decisive shortcomings in all three core areas of tank design. Albeit an impressive technology at the time, there was a long way to go.

Cambrai was seminal because the plan also embraced such a high degree of *coordination*. Different arms sought to complement each other by playing to strengths. In theory, this was nothing new on a battlefield but here it was realized with the orchestration of some groundbreaking technologies: fighter ground attack, tanks and unregistered artillery. Doctrine for tank/infantry cooperation had been supported by training. Signals and logistics components were augmented by wireless and sledge tanks. All these enhancements enabled an offensive operation to be launched against prepared defences with complete surprise, heralding the potential for operational manoeuvre and shock action. In the conceptual domain, it is possible to acknowledge the German contribution too: the *Gruppe* system, a decentralized command culture that bred initiative; *Stosstruppen* tactics espousing discrete application of firepower and envelopment. In this vein, Cambrai was a truly auspicious occasion and can justly be labelled the birth of armoured warfare.

Notwithstanding a tendency to sound wise after the event, Colonel J. F. C. Fuller went on to become one of the foremost exponents of armoured manoeuvre warfare. He was widely read by the architects of 1930s German offensive doctrine, later known as blitzkrieg. (Tank Museum 1380/A6)

THE BATTLEFIELD TODAY

For much the same reason as Cambrai was desirable to the offensive planners of Third Army, it lends itself well to physical exploration. In view of the fact that its rolling countryside had not been churned into a desolate quagmire, the ground you survey now is not at all dissimilar from that which was fought over back in 1917. Woods have maintained their original dimensions and urban development in the area has been limited – only the A26 *Autoroute* has altered the topography. The Canal du Nord is now full of water (though with the disruption caused by two world wars this did not occur until 1963).

Cambrai is a pleasant town but short on hotels. The obvious place to stay is Hotel Béatus, owned by the author of *Following the Tanks*, Philippe Gorczynski. Instrumental in the recovery of D51 'Deborah' at Flesquières in 1999, he will certainly be able to answer most specific questions you have about the battle. Many tourists also make it a day trip from an established base at Arras, which is only about half an hour's drive away.

I would highly recommend the purchase of both 'Battleground Europe' series guidebooks on Cambrai by Jack Horsfall and Nigel Cave (see Further reading). The discerning enthusiast will also benefit from the French 1:25,000 IGN map of Cambrai Ouest (Series Blue, number 2507E). The maps in this book will provide more than enough information for a general reference but access to original mapping will be required if you are looking to study the actions of individual battalions.

Original trench positions are not readily evident except in some of the woods although squat concrete bunkers still demarcate the Siegfried Stellung around Flesquières and Banteux. It is not hard to work out where the lines were from general mapping; sighting principles whittle down the options. However, more obvious landmarks are a better place to start.

Akin to most of Cambrai's landmarks, the lock on the St Quentin Canal east of Masnières is largely unchanged. This feature of the battlefield makes for a particularly fulfilling visit. (Author's collection)

British infantry killed by shellfire. As with my title on Vimy Ridge, it is important for the violence and suffering of war to have the last word. (IWM Q 23887)

Bourlon Wood is instantly evocative, especially at the right time of year. When mist clings to undergrowth astride the muddy sunken lanes, you half expect a column of grimy Welsh infantry to squelch and jostle past you. Some shell holes are still in evidence but Plunkett's hunting lodge is no more. Moving south, the ground around Fontaine and Cantaing remains faithful to its past. A wander along the tree line of La Folie Wood will send shivers down your spine – the machine guns were masterfully sighted to dominate Fontaine's southern approaches in enfilade. Flesquières is an illuminating stop too; the significance of its reverse slope beyond will demand no explanation.

It is well worth taking some time to tackle the St Quentin Canal on foot. F22's bridge at Masnières has been replaced by a more modern structure but the locks farther east have hardly changed at all. Again, few demands are placed on the imagination to hear the din and rattle of small-arms fire reverberating across the placid grey water. Le Quennet and Le Pavé Farms are to be found up on Bonavis Ridge and, if struggling to identify old German trench positions, the support line ran along the south side of Lateau Wood there very close to the road. You are now also firmly on the axis of Rupprecht's eastern *Gruppen*. Investigation of 55th Division's positions in Banteux Ravine (known now as Vallée de Villers-Guislan) adds value to comprehension of the events on 30 November. Unfortunately, the *Autoroute* embankment at the western end has dammed it where 166th Brigade put their Vickers guns; the rest of the defile is intact. Beyond the *Autoroute* towards Gonnelieu and Villers-Guislan, you can imprint images of advancing German infantry onto the open farmland.

As with most World War I battlefields, you will come across cemeteries constantly. There is an official memorial to the campaign on the N30 Bapaume–Cambrai road. These modest resting places are always a sobering interface with the cost of war. Total British casualties at Cambrai were 47,596 with about one-third of that figure killed or missing. For their part, the Germans suffered up to 53,000 casualties. Statistics like these are difficult to relate to. In this instance the combined figure would fill a national sports stadium – just one sheaf of the terrible human harvest reaped by that deplorable war. By studying military history we honour the myriad endeavours and sacrifices that captivate us. Nonetheless, the wretched fate of so many young men must always be borne in mind. One should not allow the tranquil sense of order at those cemeteries to belie the sordid manner of their passing.

FURTHER READING

Primary sources

Cambrai enjoys a wealth of source material, most of it held at the National Archives (Public Records Office) at Kew in London. Its collection of War Office files contains copies of all the operations orders, post-operation reports and war diaries from Third Army down to each battalion. It also holds copies of the War Cabinet commissioned official enquiry. Details of how to access this material are found on the website www.nationalarchives.gov.uk.

The Tank Museum Library at Bovington holds copies of Tank Corps unit war diaries and operations orders. You will also discover a miscellany of personal letters, journals, maps and sketches to embellish official documents. Amongst them is Elles' original Special Order Number 6. A limited selection of translated German primary source material complements the collection. Log onto www.tankmuseum.co.uk and follow the links to 'Library'. Imperial War Museum London (www.iwm.org.uk) is best on trench maps but the Tank Museum Library does have a few documents of interest.

Aside from the material at the Tank Museum, German primary sources are extremely difficult to find. Allied bombing in World War II destroyed the Reichsarchiv in Potsdam. Bavarian sources survived by virtue of being held in Munich but very few Bavarian units served at Cambrai.

Secondary sources

The official histories relating to Cambrai are as follows:

Britain Miles, Captain Wilfred, *History of the Great War – Military Operations France and Belgium 1917 – The Battle of Cambrai* London, 1948

Germany Struss, Hauptman Dr Georg, *Die Tankschlacht bei Cambrai 1917* Berlin, 1929

The following selection of books offers an informative examination of the battle itself:

Cooper, Bryan, *The Ironclads of Cambrai* Cassell: London 1967

Gibot, Jean-Luc, and Gorcynski, Philippe, *Following the Tanks Cambrai* Arras, 1999

Horsfall, Jack, and Cave, Nigel, *Cambrai – The Right Hook* Leo Cooper: London, 1999

Horsfall, Jack, and Cave, Nigel, *Cambrai – Bourlon Wood* Leo Cooper: London, 2002

Moore, William, *A Wood Called Bourlon: The Cover-Up After Cambrai 1917* Leo Cooper: London, 1988

Smithers, A. J., *Cambrai – The First Great Tank Battle 1917* Leo Cooper: London, 1992

For a broader perspective on related topics:

Fletcher, David, *The British Tanks 1915–19* The Crowood Press: Marlborough, 2001

Griffith, Paddy, *Battle Tactics of the Western Front* Yale University Press: London, 1994

Holmes, Richard, *Tommy* Harper Collins: London, 2004

Jünger, Ernst, *Storm of Steel* Penguin: Harmondsworth, 2004

Keegan, John, *The First World War* Alfred A. Knopf: London, 2000

Williams, Jeffery, *Byng of Vimy* Leo Cooper: London, 1982

INDEX

References to illustrations are shown in **bold**.